DRIVEN

RISING ABOVE IT ALL

RISING ABOVE IT ALL

Michael Carrington

THIS BOOK

This Book is a personal history. The events described in this book are real, backed up by police reports, family court documentations and other legal records. Many names, except for my own, as well as several geographic, chronological, and identifying details have been changed for privacy and security reasons.

If you and I met in person at a function or a neighborhood party, you would never guess I lived through childhood abuse, and on my own since 13, surviving several near death experiences.

I don't look the part.

PREFACE

This book comes at a time when all Americans, young and old, need inspiration and hope. It is, the story of a boy tossed into society at 13, after suffering unthinkable abuses. He must think as an adult at such an early age, make his own decisions and deal with the consequences. He is entirely on his own, but unseen forces guide him. You, the reader, will feel empowered as you read about him, and admire his courage and strength. His faith and inner resolve are unmatched.

You will be moved by his sacrifices and accomplishments, a boy who wants it all and dreams big. He overcomes despair never asking himself "Why me?" There is always an inner light guiding him. This light allows him to take his anger and turn it into constructive energy, at almost every turn.

Out of his despair comes strength – the drive that will propel him on his journey and bring his many dreams to reality. He learns to love and to be loved, and most of all, to cherish his life along the way.

He is betrayed by his wife and brother, and by his best friend. He adapts constantly to change, while raising his three children, through

situations where he ought to be crushed down into nothing. He survives and embraces hardship to achieve his goals. Fear is not an option. He is willing to die for his dreams.

You will want to be a part of his story and share in the gift of living life fully, in spite of all the odds. In his latest transformation, after sacrifices' everything he has, destitute and almost broken, he recreates himself once again. He travels the world – to Russia, Bulgaria, Romania, Italy, Las Vegas – and develops and engineers some of the biggest websites in the world. From his darkest hour he builds a new life for himself. And a new passion is born when he meets a woman that only God could bring to him. In her, he receives the greatest gift of all. She is the Angel that will stand alongside him.

Theodore Roosevelt Once Said:

> *It is not the critic who counts; not the man who points out how the strong man stumbles, or where the doer of deeds could have done them better. The credit belongs to the man who is actually in the arena, whose face is marred by dust and sweat and blood; who strives valiantly; who errs, who comes short again and again, because there is no effort without error and shortcoming; but who does actually strive to do the deeds; who knows great enthusiasms, the great devotions; who spends himself in a worthy cause; who at the best knows in the end the triumph of high achievement, and who at the worst, if he fails, at least fails while daring greatly, so that his place shall never be with those cold and timid souls who neither know victory nor defeat.*

CHAPTER 1

I have just returned from a business trip to Bucharest, Rome, and several other cities in central Europe. The flight back to the States took 16 hours and I feel rested. I'm used to flying – across the country to Malibu, California; Sedona, Arizona; Florida; across to Europe or to any other place in the world I need to be at a given moment.

I call my driver, and he picks me up at the airport in Detroit. We depart for nearby Oakland, with rolling hills and dogwoods in bloom. This is one of the wealthiest counties in the country, and we pass by palatial homes that I was contracted to landscape – heavy work like installing bridges over rivers, building retaining walls, excavating through the terrain, or constructing a golf course. I design, I create , I rebuild. I almost smile at the thought, because I've had to rebuild my life many times over. The hand I've been dealt should have crushed me down to nothing. I have overcome the unthinkable.

We near my town and pass by a home that I built for myself years ago – built it and then sacrificed it. It was modeled on a youthful fantasy of mine, from the show Dynasty, with a circular driveway

made of brick pavers. More like a landing strip, measuring 220 x 40 feet, similar to Hugh Hefner's home. There are two entry gates, and another large driveway to exit.

The muscles in my arms and hands tighten as I remember all the work that took and the great satisfaction. But then I had to make a choice and rebuild again.

At certain moments, if you've looked at yourself hard enough and without bias, you can see yourself. The true image finally comes into focus. I see now that I built a fortress of material things to protect myself from ever needing again. I raised my three children alone, and this fortress was our buffer, our safety. I meant it to be.

The wheels of the car shudder slightly as we turn into my driveway. The house looks quiet. My son is out working, installing a small, man-made river on a nearby property. I thank my driver, grab my suitcase and walk inside. I take off my coat, drape it over the back of a chair and go into the kitchen to make some coffee. But once inside the room, some-thing makes me stop...the cord that runs from the coffee machine to the wall socket. I stand there, stock still, looking at that cord, and the whole event begins to replay like a film in my head...

I remember coming home from school on one late May after-noon. It was already hot in Michigan, with blue skies, sunshine, and the days were getting longer. It was a Friday and I was about to begin the first of many traumatic events. I know everyone suffers through terrible things. In my case, however, this began a series that would continue on through my later marriage.

At the time, I was happy because school was going to let out in a couple weeks for summer vacation. And I was hungry, as usual.

My mother used to shop at grocery stores that would offer triple coupons towards merchandise. She used to buy alot and she would

put it in this big freezer that we had in the basement. Food didn't last long in my house, not with four boys there, but I wasn't eating more than my share of it, but it would always seem to disappear. So, she started locking the freezer. She would also lock me out of the house to "save" food. Most the time, though, my brothers George, John and David were responsible.

When I got home this sunny day, I was locked out again. My three brothers were inside because David, who was a year younger than me, had the key that Mom gave him. Later, I found out that he would always make sure he was home before me so he could keep me out.

That didn't bother me. I was a skinny kid then and could crawl in the basement window to get in the house. The window was always hard to lock so it was open most of the time. The window was only 12" x 36", but I was tiny enough to fit through.

Unfortunately, the doors from the basement were locked. There were two of them: one led to the bedroom; the other, to the kitchen. David, George and John would always make sure that both doors stayed locked when our mother was gone. I would beg them to open the door. John and George were really too young. I think they were more scared than anything else. They just did what our mom said. They didn't want to end up like me. I never blamed them, but I did blame and hate David. I would beg them to let me in to get something to eat and get a shower. George and John did sometimes. David never would.

I was stuck inside this day. I don't know what time it was when Mom came home from work, but I remember the sun was going down. I could see long shadows in the yard – the longest of my life, foretelling the event that would cause deep and permanent changes.

As my mother came into the house, I could hear her walking upstairs on the floor. I didn't say a word. David told her I was downstairs. I heard her coming towards the door, and then the click of the lock. I hid in the corner between the couch and the wall. I didn't say a word. I was hoping she wouldn't find me.

She didn't. I knew she was looking for me, but, after walking around, she went back upstairs. I thought I was safe, but I was wrong. Then she came back down. I couldn't get back behind the couch quick enough. When I did, I moved the couch, causing a squeak.

Mom came over to the couch and grabbed me by the arm. I saw that she had a coffee cord in her hand. She held me down with one hand and began beating me with a coffee cord in the other. I kept begging her to stop. She was screaming and yelling as she was whipping me, telling me to stay out of the house and don't ever come back in the house again when the doors were locked.

Then, I started getting mad. Something told me I wasn't going to take this anymore. I tried to get away from my mother. She leaned over and grabbed a swing set chain that was on the floor in the basement next to one of the concrete support columns that held up the first floor with a steel beam.

She threw me on the ground, wrapped the chain around me and tied me to the pole. Then, she went upstairs then to get a lock. She came back down, thudding hard on the stairs, and locked the chains together. It happened so quickly and, I couldn't believe what she had done. I was in a state of disbelief. My heart raced as I fought back, but it was useless. I couldn't escape from the chains or pull down the column.

I started screaming for my life. My little heart was beating faster and faster. Tears streamed down my face. I could feel welts and

bruises all over my body. My head was throbbing and hurting so bad. I thought she was going to kill me. I had nothing to protect my face. I had held my head down so she couldn't hit me in the face with the coffee cord, but she did manage to catch me in the neck a couple times. The pain, the stinging, was so unbearable.

Then I started yelling that I should be living with my father. They had gotten divorced when I was only 2. My father would have never tied me to a pole, I screamed. I kept saying my dad was better than she was because he would never treat me like this and beat me.

My mother came back. Her face was red; her eyes, wild. She yanked at my shirt and pulled it off. My pants followed with a savage pull. Then, she started flailing again with the coffee cord. I tried to shield myself to bend away from the cord, but I had no place to hide. I was screaming and yelling now for help. I begged her to stop. I couldn't move. When I finally gave up, I just lay there, perfectly still. She beat me so hard that I became numb to the pain.

I thought I was better off dead. I was dying. She whipped me so hard for so long and I was in so much pain and with welts and bruises all over my body, I didn't think I would live to see the next day. I whispered to her with the little strength I had left, "Go ahead and kill me."

Then, from somewhere, I heard the voice of God. All of a sudden, he answered me. It was the voice I had heard before when I was a little kid. He told me I would be watched after, that he was with me and that nothing would happen to me. Then, I felt at peace. Something came over me as I was crying and hurting. Something just came and sat beside me and said, "Don't get mad. I am with you. It is I who will judge and punish." I asked: why did I deserve this? I heard what I thought the answer was: "You are my child. You have to

endure pain and suffering before you can realize life like I once did." Now, I thought, this was Jesus. I knew I had the power to get through the beating.

God is going to get you back, I told my mother. He will pay you back for what you have done here today. In reply, she beat me harder.

I could hear someone upstairs. I didn't know who it was, but I figured it was one of my aunts or uncles because nobody would come over to the house anyway. My mother didn't have any friends. I wouldn't find out who it was that showed up that day until I was an adult.

There was nothing anyone could do anyway. Besides, all my relatives had their own families to worry about. I was ashamed enough to have a mother who was capable of inflicting such horrific punishment on a child, let alone her own son. She had already whipped me to exhaustion. She heard the footsteps above and stopped. I am sure, if someone hadn't shown up at that time, my mother probably would have killed me.

My mother then went upstairs and locked the doors behind her. I had some strength left. I screamed to whoever was on the first floor that God would pay back my mother, that she had beaten me. No one came down. I sat there tied up with no clothes, beaten, badly bruised and exhausted. I passed that night just like that.

The next morning, I managed to wiggle out of the chains and free myself. I was alive, but badly bruised and probably scarred at this point with welts all over me. I thought these were not going to go away by the time I had to return to school on Monday. I didn't know what to do. I was always thinking of going to school because it was the only way to get away from her and this house.

The upstairs doors were unlocked. I crept back to my room and got dressed. My mother never said anything to me at all. It was like nothing ever happened.

There was only a few weeks left of school. I had to figure out was going to cover myself up so no one would know I was beaten. That would not be easy with bruises, and welts the size of tomatoes all over my arms, legs, stomach and back. Luckily, it was still cool enough to wear a long-sleeve shirt and pants.

I had another problem: how would I hide my right hand, which I used to try to block the coffee cord from hitting my face? I could barely move my hand. I thought it was broken. I would have to make up a story that I fell off my bike.

Most of the neighbors already knew what was going on in our house, but the ones next door didn't know what to do; they didn't really want to get involved. I thought they would call the police. Back then, nobody knew who to call to stop child abuse. I thought this was not right, that this shouldn't be allowed. I knew I was being abused.

I would find out later that week that the neighbors did hear me down in the basement, yelling and screaming for help. I didn't know that my best friends, Michael and Chris, were watching through the basement window as my mom beat me. I told nobody. They were in shock. They told their parents what had happened. So then, after that night, they told me that if I ever needed a place to stay that I could come over and stay the night. Eric, my other friend down the street, lived next to Chris and learned of what happened from Mike and Chris. He made the same offer. I would truly find out how blessed I was to have the friends and neighbors and their parents. I could not have felt more ashamed from that moment on: my friends knew what my mother was like.

I lost a mother that day. I would lose any kind of love and feelings I had for her, all respect I had for her, forever. This was not my mother. This was something evil, and I did not love it. I would never be the same. I had no mother. I was so ashamed and embarrassed that I didn't have a normal family. Not only was I without a father, now. I was motherless, too.

I think George and John were so scared of my mother even they knew whipping me like that was wrong. So, they would do everything my mother told them to do even if it meant locking the doors to keep me out of the house in subzero wintry weather, even if I kept telling them I could die out here if they didn't let me in. That's how scared they were of our mother. David, of course, didn't care.

I didn't blame them. I knew they didn't understand, and I didn't want them to be whipped and beaten like me. I did love my brothers, but I had to survive. All I had was God on my side and the voice that kept telling me I've been okay. I made it to the end of the school year. I had managed to cover up the bruises and welts. I wore long-sleeved shirts even though I looked a little ridiculous. They were hot, but the disguise worked. Nobody ever knew or found out in school what had happened to me other than my close friends, who never said anything to anyone.

We had a couple days of school left when I had come home to find my mom there. I noticed another car in the driveway. I didn't recognize this car or know who it belonged to.

Inside the house, I found two African-American women talking to my mother. One introduced herself to me as Donna. The other was Tina. They had come from the state Department of Human Services.

While Donna was talking to my mom, George and John played on the couch. David was nowhere in sight. He always seemed to disappear when something was going on, but he sure did know how to get me in trouble. Tina went around the house, looking in the cupboards and the bedrooms. Donna then asked me where I slept. I showed Tina my bedroom.

After returning to the living room, I asked the women what is this all about. They said they wanted to make sure that there was enough food in the house, and that we had enough clothes and were dressed properly. They said that somebody had called their office to report yelling and screaming as if somebody were dying. They were required to investigate every report. They were not allowed to tell us who had called or exactly what they said. Only later did I discover that our neighbors, the Sebastian's, had called social services.

I thought: should I tell the women what's going on? I still have a few marks on my body to prove that my mom was abusing me. But then I thought, if these people leave, I am going to be beaten again. How could they protect me? I was too young to understand. I thought Mom would kill me. I was just too scared. I didn't quite have enough courage to reveal the truth at this point, and I still had to go to school. Where would I go to school? Or what would they do to me?

I wouldn't take the chance. I didn't know what would happen. I just didn't know the women would then leave the house and say that they would make a report. I was thinking that if I was beaten ever again, my mother would be in big trouble and go to jail.

However, back then, they really didn't do anything about child abuse it was more or less viewed as a minor social problem They just cared about if the kids were fed and clothed properly.

Still, after the women left, my mom seemed to be less inclined to beat me or whip me. I think she got scared a little bit, but this would be short-lived, as I was to find out. I never retaliated against my mother. I couldn't — she was much bigger than me.

I knew enough to never hit my mother. Nor did I ever try to even raise a hand towards her. I would always run from her. I wasn't supposed to hit girls, anyway. I knew that. Otherwise, I would have the whole family coming down on me.

What I couldn't understand was why she would beat me like she did.

When school ended, I got to see a couple of my aunts and uncles, but I would never tell them what happened that day, down in the basement, until I was an adult. By then, I had the courage and felt no shame. I knew who I was. And I always knew that it wasn't my fault.

Knowing that, helps when I look back at my tormented life.

My Aunt Lucy, who I didn't see often, started talking to me a little bit about my father. She told me how mean he was and how my mother kept me from him because of his behavior. She said that he beat her and was an alcoholic. She also said I looked so much like him, especially when I got mad. When I was angry I looked just like him.

CHAPTER 2

1961. A Libra, I was born on October 11th to Connie and Clarence Pickle, I was named after St.Michael the Archangel. It was a quiet month as far as the world goes. Roger Maris hit a then-record 61 homeruns, beating Babe Ruth's record. John F. Kennedy became our 35th president this year, and, oddly enough, our 44th president, Barack Obama, was born in August of this same year. I entered the world without much fanfare. Soon after I was born, my brother David was born on April 11, 1963. Not long after, my mother ended up divorcing my father.

We lived in a pretty big house in Michigan with my mother's mother and father, Vonda and Irvin Stevens. David and I were little ones: I was 2; he was 1 when we moved into my grandparents' home.

My grandfather was very nice, although he was gone most of the time to drive a truck and haul cars. Later on, he started working for Great Lakes Steel on these big electrical generators, which were so big and so loud they eventually took my grandfather's hearing. My grandmother was a housewife. I don't remember her ever working

outside the home. She watched me and David all the time, and was busy raising her own kids.

They had a pretty large family, all girls, including a set of twins. They were my aunts. The youngest of the five girls was my Aunt Lisa. She was still in high school then. After coming home from school, she would sometimes watch me and my brother David. That was always fun. I really didn't get to see much of the twins, Aunt Lucy and Aunt Cathy, or Aunt Marion. They were too busy working or going to school. All I know is those girls sure did fight a lot and argue. It seemed like every day somebody was arguing about something.

One night, I woke up to a lot of commotion yelling and screaming. I got up to see what was wrong: somebody had thrown a brick through the picture window of the house. My aunts told me to go upstairs. I did, but, while upstairs, I looked out the window into the backyard to find out what was going on, and I saw somebody crawling next to the garage in the backyard on his hands and knees. I thought somebody had done something very bad, but didn't know what.

This was very strange to remember, and I remember the event like it happened yesterday. Then, I saw two people were arguing on the front porch. I know now one was my soon-to-be Uncle Charlie, who was arguing with my father, who had thrown the brick. I never really knew my father, but, after that night, I wondered why he would do such a thing. I couldn't believe it. Afterwards, I overheard somebody in the family saying he just wanted to see my mother and me.

I never knew until later in life that it is unusual to have the kind of a memory that allows me to remember all the way back to 2 years old and recall everything that happened throughout my life in great detail. When I think about something – anything, really – a picture comes into my mind like I am watching a movie. If something

happened to me, I can remember everything about it. Later on in life, I realized I had a photographic memory.

I know this is a gift and continue to use it to my advantage. . (To this day I can watch something done once and duplicate it. I have this skill – seeing something once and being able to do it.)

After that night on the front porch, I did not hear from nor see my father again for a few years. Growing up with my grandparents, I never really saw my mother much either. She was too busy working all the time for Ford Motor Co. in Rawsonville, Michigan.

Growing up in my grandfathers and grandmothers house wasn't the easiest. It was only a three-bedroom Colonial. On the other hand, Thanksgiving, Christmas, Easter and our birthdays were the fun times. Thanksgiving, the food, Wow! When my aunts' boyfriends and friends of the family showed up, we'd sit down at a huge table for a Thanksgiving dinner. It was a lot of fun, and, boy, did we eat the turkey along with the dressing, mashed potatoes, sweet potatoes and you name it. We really enjoyed listening to all the stories the soon-to-be uncles would tell.

Christmas was the best. Every year a different aunt and uncle would have Christmas at their house. Every Christmas, we would always put milk and cookies out for Santa Claus and try to catch him coming at night. We never caught Santa Claus, but always found the milk and cookies gone. I remember one year getting a train set. It was so cool. I always shared and let my brother play with it. Eventually, he stopped asking for permission to play with the train set and ended up breaking some pieces. He was always breaking my gifts. Also, one year, we received some hats, scarves and gloves. We also got a lot of games, like Mousetrap and Doctor.

Everybody was different around the holidays, and I never figured out why they couldn't act this way all year long with no one yelling at each other and just grateful that we were all together. I always wondered why my family couldn't always be like this every day instead of just a couple of times a year.

That was just another series of questions I asked myself. When you're a kid, you really don't know anything. You just wonder, watch and ask yourself a bunch of questions. If you ask them out loud, adults seem to think you're stupid or something, but you're really not. They treat you like a little kid who knows nothing. That's what my mother and grandmother did. On the other hand, you think you know everything, but you don't. You don't realize what parents have to go through to raise you. You don't realize what it takes to put food on the table.

You don't realize what their struggles are in life being parents just to make sure you have clothes on your back, shoes on your feet and a roof over your head. I didn't even realize that I had to depend on my parents.

Kids just basically become attached to their parents because they were born there. They have nowhere else to go, or know what to do, or how to get away from them.

Easter was good to my family, too. Friends of my aunts and uncles would come over. They would bring big baskets full of all sorts of candy and chocolate bunnies. Naturally, we would always eat too much and didn't feel too good afterwards. We would also sit down with family and friends at the dinner table on Easter. We only had a cooked ham, I guess it was a family tradition.

On the other hand, I couldn't wait to be an adult just to get out of this insane madhouse with so many people crammed together.

Birthdays were great with all the presents, but my brother liked to play with the gifts, and would always break them. Then, I would have nothing.

Still, I learned early in life how to be happy without material objects or love. More importantly, I discovered how to be happy with the beauty that surrounded me. I was able to use my surroundings and environment – what I had available to me – to create that moment, the adventure, the fantasy, the dream and bring it to life. I could escape, find fun and happiness. And, it was free. A staircase and a banister that led to the upstairs, cardboard boxes we used to slide down the staircase like a sled on snow: that was so much fun. There was a big cherry tree out in the backyard. David and I used to climb the tree all the time, and, of course, we got into trouble because, even when we were told not to, we did anyway. If my grandmother caught us, she would swat us with a tree branch from that cherry tree. That really hurt.

If we said a bad word or a bad name – we all know what those words are – she would be quick with a bar of soap to wash out our mouths. That was horrible. If my brother said a bad word, he sometimes blamed me. I would always get the soap in the mouth; sometimes, I got the soap and the tree branch. My grandmother seemed to take great joy in swatting me with a stick and shoving soap down my throat. I did not like her at all.

While growing up, David and I would play hide and seek. He would never find me. I had my secret hiding place where I could go and nobody could find me. Most of the time, I went to my hiding place after getting in trouble and being disciplined by my grandmother. It was an escape from reality, and I knew I was safe there.

When I did decide to tell someone about it, I told my Aunt Lisa. I could trust her. To get there, I would walk down the staircase to the

basement. On the side of the wall, there was an opening. I would squeeze inside. Aunt Lisa couldn't believe I fit because the space was so tiny. Still, I did.

I didn't realize it then, but I was inside the wall of the house. There was a fire extinguisher hanging on the wall beside the staircase, and a clothes chute. It led to the third floor of the house, but wasn't in use.

I could climb all the way upstairs through the chute. I used to take a flashlight up there and sometimes a book with me so I wouldn't be scared. When someone called me, I would crawl down. The person who wanted me would ask me where I was. I'd say I was going to the bathroom or downstairs washing my hands, whatever suited the moment. I felt like a superhero in the comic books, and I liked comic books, especially almighty Thor, the Norse god of thunder and son of Odin, lord of the gods. He was my favorite.

I needed a place to hide. As I grew up, I realized my grandmother and mother didn't like me so much, if at all. I found out not too many people liked my grandmother at all either. Soon, I was being blamed for everything and was in trouble all the time.

David seemed to think it was funny how he would get away with everything and that I would be punished. My brother started to take great joy if he could get away with something. It became a game to get me in trouble. As hard as I tried to stay out of trouble, I always seemed to get in trouble.

I just wanted out: no family and no brother. The only times I would be happy would be during the holidays, but they came around only once a year.

With all the abuse, however, I never really felt close to my parents. Often, I didn't even feel part of the family.

CHAPTER 3

I was about eight years old when my mother beat me. The years before that actually had some bright spots, but were marked by too much abuse. My mother's attack was the culmination of the problems, not a lone event. Besides, she wasn't the only one in the family aiming at me.

My grandmother was constantly hitting me with a branch from the cherry tree in the backyard or washing out my mouth with soap. David would watch, laughing at me most of the time. My grandmother would just ask him to stop, but she never hit him or forced soap into his mouth.

Only much later did I find out why David was the family pet. At a young age, my brother had been near death with a respiratory problem. He had become dehydrated and almost died. My mother didn't think he would make it. Aunt Cathy came home one day and saw that David was having problems. He just didn't seem right and said we needed to take him to the hospital. He would have died if he were not taken to the hospital that day. David came through the ordeal, but my family was always fearful that something could happen to him

again. So, he was always babied and spoiled. Grandmother Vanda started favoring him. So did my mother. They kept favoring him throughout their lives. He could do nothing wrong. He could lie, cheat and steal right in front of your face and make everyone believe that he had never done anything wrong. This led him to believe that he could be this way all through his life. And he became good at it.

Fortunately, I also had idealized images of my father to sustain me. Of course, my mother kept me pretty far away from my real father. I thought my father would never allow the swatting, spanking and washing my mouth out with soap to continue.

At times, I wondered if I'd survive. Even as a child, I realized that I had to get out of there or I was going to end up dead.

Still, there was something that brought me pleasure. I can remember sleeping in the living room in my grandmother's and grandfather's house. David and I would always fight over who would get to sleep on the couch. My grandmother would again take charge and make that decision. I guess, since it was my grandmother's house, she made all the decisions.

I like the couch because, there, I would always hear the grandfather clock going off every hour. For some reason, this was very comforting to me. I soon realized that the clock reminded me I was still alive. That was weird, waking up to some clock going off in the middle of the night and thinking I'm alive. That was a later realization. I didn't understand it then, but I do now. I was afraid of the next day coming and how much trouble I would be in.

As a child, I didn't really understand anything. I depended on others, both adults and family. I felt hopelessly unloved and unwanted. I couldn't do anything about the situation while I was under their control. In such distress, the grandfather clock comforted me.

Then, something inside me told me that I shouldn't be afraid. This was the same voice that helped endure my mother's savage beating. I don't know what it was, but late one night, I woke up at the sound of the grandfather clock going off—ding, ding, ding. Then, I heard a voice telling me everything will be okay; "I am watching over you." I started thinking after a while it was ghosts or I was hearing things. I didn't know and was a little scared, but then I thought that these were comforting words that were not harmful to me. They were nice.

These words later on gave me strength to live. It was something deep down inside of me that comforted me after that night. I didn't know what it was, but I wanted to find out. I didn't know how to. So, one day, I was up in my secret hiding place between the walls, and I just kept thinking and asking myself what was going on. All of a sudden, I heard the voice again. I was scared. I had heard of ghosts in some of the books that Aunt Lisa had read to me. I didn't know what to think. The voice said again, "You will be okay. Nothing will happen to you. I am watching over you. Be strong." I didn't know what it was, but it was very comforting to me.

I didn't know what was going to happen to me from day to day. I started talking to myself to get through this nightmare that I was living in. Was I crazy? I don't think so. Still, I did not dare tell anybody about the voice, but Aunt Lisa's dog, Heidi. She was a purebred German shepherd. She was all black and medium-sized. The females are always the smaller in that breed. Heidi was the greatest. She was like part of the family. Heidi was a female and was very well mannered. She would do everything that she was told: sit, lie down and so on. My brother and I were so small that we always tried to ride Heidi like a horse. That was fun, but we ended up in trouble if we tried. So,

I didn't try that too often. She protected us. I loved Heidi. She was my friend, the only one that never hurt me, we shared many special moments together.

Thank goodness, Heidi was never abused, beaten or soap down her throat or yelled at. Heidi always had food and water. The dog was treated better than me.

I also always felt close to my Aunt Lisa. When everyone had gone out, she would babysit us. Since she was still in school, I think she could relate to us. She was a breath of fresh air, looking forward to her reading to us all kinds of stories. Then there was the Dairy Queen down at the corner of Wynona where she would take me and my brother for a treat.

About that time, things did change. In 1964, my mother met a man named Bob Sneed , who would soon become my new father. Bob worked at Ford Motor Company with my mother and started doing a lot of things with us. My mom was happy when we went to the local lake to go fishing together. We did all the normal things a family would do together. Best of all, David couldn't fool our new father.

As a father, Bob was very fair and smart, and treated David and me as if we were his own two sons.

His arrival heralded even better news. One day, my mother came home and said that they had purchased a new home. Then, we moved to a three-bedroom house in Taylor, Michigan with a base-ment, garage and a big backyard. This was a great house. Everything seemed to be going much better after such hardships. I hoped I would get my own room, but no such luck. David and I slept in bunk beds. Bob said David would get the top bunk one month; then I would get the top bunk the next month.

Not much bad happened when Bob was around. I thought he was a very smart man and a good disciplinarian. He was fair and honest. He always explained his actions if we did get in trouble, telling us why we were in trouble and what the punishment would be.

Most of the time, he sent us to our rooms. When it came to fun activities, he always did whatever he promised to do with us unless we were in trouble and basically grounded. He took the time and effort to set us down and show us right from wrong. I loved my new father.

We even went on a vacation. I had no idea what a vacation was, but it sounded nice since we were all going as a family. Bob took us to a lake with a cottage on it. We went there for a couple of days. We had so much fun, and I never got in trouble. We played around the lake every day. I remember the long, wooden boat dock. We'd go to the end of it and jump off. Today, I know the place as Walled Lake. We'd put on lifejackets, and Father would sometimes throw us into the lake. There were a couple of swings that we always used to play on. We shared an inner tube too, and took turns pushing each other off it.

I thought that this was the life. It was a great way to cool off during hot summer days in August. Everything was perfect: blue skies, lots of sun and fresh air. I was finally loving who I was and wanting to live every day. If every day was like these days, I thought I would be really happy.

Of course, it couldn't last.

As I got ready to start school, my mother had a baby, George. A tiny little thing, he was always whining, always wanting something. I didn't get much sleep those days, but I felt so proud that I had a baby brother.

A year later, I had another brother, John. My mother was happy, too, so Bob must have loved her and treated her like she wanted to be treated. For the short time they were together, my parents raised me and David with my other two brothers the same.

I have always considered George and, John as my real brothers. I never called them stepbrothers.

I finally had a father. My biological father, Clarence, was never a father. As an alcoholic, he really couldn't be. He would lose control of himself. That explains why my mother kept us so disconnected from him and his family.

In time, Bob would leave us.

CHAPTER 4

I didn't go to public school. I was sent to St. Paschal's, a nearby Catholic school. Until then, I had not been raised with any religion. We never went to church, and I had learned little about Christianity. I knew about Christmas, of course, but that was for gifts, big meals and family get-togethers.

I think we lived around 2 to 3 miles from the school. One day that I remember quite well, my mother walked me down the street about a block or two in a pouring rainstorm. There was this big yellow bus waiting for me, idling by the curb and filled with strange kids. I got on alone. David was still too young for school. My mother said I had to go, even though the idea scared me. I can still see all the eyes turning to stare at me as I edged up the big steps and turned by the driver's seat to face these many strangers. Unfortunately, I really never made any new friends at this school. I don't know why. I guess I was just shy and scared, and really afraid of trouble.

Besides, school was a really strange place. When the bus arrived at school, I was stunned to see the bus greeted by people in robes with ropes for belts. I didn't know anything about monks, nuns or priests.

I only knew these people didn't look like anyone in my neighborhood. Some of them seemed to be wearing dresses. They wore big hats, which appeared to have wings. That was weird enough, but they also had big silver chains with this big silver thing that looked to me like two knives stuck together, forming, I guess, another plane. I was the one taking off on my educational career, but they looked ready to fly.

I had never seen anyone like this. I heard some stories about people from outer space, probably from television cartoons or stories Aunt Lisa read us. These people looked like Martians. I did not know what to expect.

My teacher was called Sister Anita. Naturally, I wondered whose sister she was. She took us to church, which was a new experience for me. As we walked down the hall to go to church, I didn't know what to expect. I heard creepy organ music playing as we entered a large building with colored glass and images of people etched into the glass. I thought they were flying, too. There were lots of candles burning everywhere. I decided we were on a spaceship, and I would never go home again. I asked Sister Anita what this was, and she said it was the place where God resides. That sounded plausible and a lot better than a UFO.

We sat down on long pews. A man dressed in a robe like Sister Anita walked up to us carrying this silver thing that looked like a rod. He didn't have a flying hat. He had the big silver chain around his neck with those two knives hanging from it. Later, I learned the knives were actually a cross. The priest also had a band around his neck that was black with a white square in the middle. I thought it was a very strange tie.

The priest put the metal rod to his mouth and spoke to us in a loud voice. I realized later the rod was a microphone. At the time, I wondered if he were the God that Anita had talked about. He definitely was loud. His voice echoed around the church.

His presence led to more questions for Sister Anita. She told me that the priest was not God, but merely spreading the word of God. That was very hard to decipher at the time. My focus was elsewhere anyway. I thought that the school day seemed to stretch forever, that I had been abducted by these people and that I would never go home again.

Finally, however, the bus dropped me off near my house. I asked my parents about the people at school, and they echoed Sister Anita's comments about school and the priest. However, David said they were aliens. I believed him.

I didn't have friends at school, but found more than enough in the neighborhood. They knew about the school, too, and told me it was more strict and disciplined than the public school. They also knew about God, which surprised me. Everyone else seemed to know about God except me.

I wasn't doing very well at St. Pascal's. I couldn't pay attention because I was always distracted. Once we started learning the alphabet, painting and cutting things out things with scissors, there really wasn't much time to play, although they did have a recess. Besides, this place frightened me. Eventually, though, I discovered T-ball.

During recess, I watched some kids playing on a big field. They would swing a bat at a ball placed on a stand and then run around. I wanted to play, but I knew nothing about it. To be honest, I had no idea what they were doing. Like the word God, I had heard about it,

but it was still only a word. Some kids called their game baseball, and that was good enough for me.

After I got up enough courage, I had asked some older kids what was going on. They told me how the game was being played. Funny thing is I remembered every word they told me on the game. I really liked what I was seeing. There were kids standing in the infield. Some kids would go up to the home plate, and there was this pedestal there made of rubber. An adult would place the ball on top of this rubber pedestal. The batter hit the ball off of that pedestal. Kids in the infield would run to get the ball in and throw the ball over to a base to get the batter out. I just didn't know how to join.

One day at recess, I saw my next-door neighbor, Mike Sebastian, playing T-ball. I was happy to see someone that I could talk to. Besides, we have the same first name. I asked Michael how he got to play T-ball, and he said his mom and dad got him into playing and that he was on a team. I just needed to get my parents to sign me up.

My parents talked to the priest, and everyone agreed that playing T-ball might help me concentrate more. So I started playing the game with my friend, Michael. Unfortunately, it didn't change my academic abilities. Of course, my failures led to mistreatment.

When I did something wrong at school, Sister Anita would put me in a corner on a chair with a dunce hat after embarrassing me in front of the whole class. She would also slap me with a yard-stick. Her form of punishment was different from my grand-mother's but just as distasteful. She just wanted to humiliate me and make me feel 2 inches tall in front of the whole class. Her treatment of me didn't seem to sound like the behavior of some-one who follows God's word. She said, "Love my neighbor, be nice to people and honor thy father and mother," but did just the

opposite of what she was teaching us. She must have thought kids were stupid, that they have no feelings or they can't figure it out. I could. I wanted out of this school. They were doing just the opposite of what they were teaching us. Then, I realized later on when I was a little older that they were nothing but hypocrites, nothing more than people who were putting out a false appearance of virtue or religion. Basically, they were not who they said they were if they were acting like this. At least, this is the way I felt. David was right: these people were Martians.

Years later, when I thought about my experience at St. Paschal's, I finally realized I was not with a bunch of aliens, but with nuns and priests committed in the belief in the Word of God and that Jesus Christ gave his life for all of our sins.

My mom and dad wanted me and my brother to attend this school so we could learn about God and who He was. However, when I finally thought I had found the answers to my questions, I discovered more questions continue to pop up and have for the rest of my life. There are no easy answers.

However, I discovered in time that going to church and learning about God, attending catechism and making all my sacraments got me through some of my toughest times.

I also had learned that being named after the greatest archangel of all, St. Michael. Michael means, "Who is like God?" The prophet Daniel (12:1) wrote, "Michael the great prince who shall rise at the time of the end."[10] He is the supreme enemy of Satan and the fallen angels, who vanquished Satan and ejected him from Paradise. At the final hour of the final battle, he will ask rhetorically and scornfully, who is like God? as he slays Satan. He is the Christian angel of death. Another role of Michael's is the weighing of souls. As

a result, the archangel is often depicted as holding scales. As such, Michael symbolizes the victory of good over evil.

Having , the leader of the army of God like Michael, the Archangel, on my side helped save my life. That's what the voice was telling me. I felt comfort when I heard the voice tell me that everything will be okay. I eventually understood someone or something with more power than anyone had on this earth was truly watching over me.

Knowing this gave me great strength, courage and faith for I was now very proud of my name, Michael. Later in life, I would become the rescuer.

CHAPTER 5

During my first year at St. Pascal's, I concentrated on T-ball and got very good at it. Unfortunately, Sister Anita and the priests weren't happy with my progress in class. My grades were poor, but they were good enough to go on to first grade or so I thought.

Actually, instead, my parents held me back a year and moved me to Blair Moody Elementary, a public school. Fortunately, because I started kindergarten before my fifth birthday, I was able to repeat kindergarten and not be that much older than my classmates.

While St. Paschal's wasn't particularly large, Blair Moody was huge. That didn't bother me as much as losing T-ball.

My religious education picked up, too. We had started going as a family to St. Cyril of Jerusalem Catholic Church, a very big place. I suppose this is what my parents wanted, so I went along with it. I was really curious anyway and really did learn a lot. St. Cyril Church would be our church for a long time to come. I attended catechism with David and completed my sacraments to become Catholic. At church, I also learned about God and the Devil, whose existence raised a lot more unanswered questions. The Devil is evil. God is

good in all things. There is more evil on this earth than good. I have been living in it with my mother and grandmother. I knew what evil was. I knew what hell was, too. God in heaven represented the good in life. For the first time, I had knowledge, power and faith. I hoped it would be enough to help me survive.

When I went to church, I felt God's presence. That made me feel whole and happy. In God, the holy father of life and all living things, I had a friend who would always protect me. As, I got older and the priests and nuns were abusing kids, my views would change. My faith would not.

I was also happier in public school. I remember getting up every morning and going to kindergarten. At Blair Moody, there were no flying nuns. We got to play a lot on the playground for recess, and there was a lot to do there: slides, swings, merry-go-rounds and teeter-totters. This is still what all kids love to do. These kinds of games didn't exist at St. Paschal's. Besides, I was too shy and scared to play with the kids there. Not at Blair Moody.

My teacher, Alice Scott, was great. One thing I remember about Miss Scott was that she was so willing to help, and she didn't yell at us kids. She was very nice. I also made a couple of new friends, Joe Brady and John Haydock.

For some strange reason, a couple of girls, Karen and Michelle, wanted to play with us. Being boys, we really didn't know what to think of these girls. We just thought that girls should get out of our way and stay away. They seemed kind of weird. I soon found out these girls were pretty cool. Karen and Michelle had very soft, comforting voices. I kind of wanted to hang around with them, but I did what the other boys did. I stayed away. All the other kids usually talked about them behind their back. I didn't like them saying bad

things about Karen and Michelle. As I got older, I realized that was wrong. I didn't know it then, but Michelle and Karen would become my best friends throughout all my school years into high school.

Then, one day, Bob was gone. I don't remember exactly what had happened. My mother never told me. All she did tell me was that he was a gambler. He liked to go to the race tracks, and he would lose all his money there.

My mother would never be the same again. She would get very angry. Whenever, I brought up my father's name, I would get slapped, punched, hit with a wooden spoon and then locked up in my room. This kind of punishment would only get worse years to come. She would resort to other methods of whipping and abusing me as I got older.

Her treatment of me would be the turning point in my life. I would take no more punishment from anyone in this family. I began treating my mother and grandmother like they treated me, and talking to them as they talked to me.

I also started to stick up for myself and look for ways to be stronger bigger and faster. Although I was just 6 going on 7, the beatings would get only worse and more often. My mother would resort to using the unthinkable methods to inflict pain and punishment. I would just get stronger and faster. So, when I would watch superheroes on TV, I would try to pretend I was one of them: Batman, Spiderman, the Incredible Hulk and the Almighty Thor.

Although I didn't have any money or a way to buy things, I figured out that I would just start lifting anything and everything that was heavy. I lifted my bike over fence. My mom always kept a chain around the fence gate and kept it locked, so I would always have to lift my bike over it. It was so heavy, but it made me stronger. I would

lift anything that was heavy to get myself stronger. Then, when I played baseball, I felt like I was Superman running down the bases. I would get faster and faster.

That's about all I could do to make the best of the situation. Mom had to find some way to have someone watch us, so she hired a babysitter named Ann. She quickly became a permanent fixture in our lives. Ann was related to the family on my grandfathers' side.

That should have alerted me. If my grandmother was the wicked witch of the West, Ann's bailiwick was the North.

Whenever I would get into trouble with her, she would lock us in the room with no food or water. She wouldn't even let me go to the bathroom. One time, I ended up crapping myself. I can laugh now, but, then, it wasn't too funny. David sometimes got locked in with me, but not often. He always tried to make sure that I was always at fault for whatever happened.

Unfortunately, home life was deteriorating. Food was becoming scarce. If you didn't eat when the food was there, you didn't eat at all. I soon learned why. My mother was laid off from the Ford Motor Co. We would eventually end up going to social services and on welfare for a long time. It would be many years before she ended up going back to Ford to work. I remember going to pick up food stamps so she could shop for food. She would also receive a check once a month to help pay bills. My mother had a hard time raising us. Food and clothing were going to be difficult to come by. I was six years old at the time.

Things would never get better, only worse. Since my mom was unemployed, my grandmother started visiting more. Strangely, Grandfather Steven's also started coming over to the house. Everyone liked him. He was nice but he was strict. He never said a bad

thing to anyone or anybody in the family. As far as I knew, he got along with everybody. My grandfather was a hard worker. I remember he would always come over and fix something that broke, including the washer or dryer or some appliance. Later on, I realized my grandmother and grandfather were divorced, but they would still talk to each other.

Eventually, my grandmother moved to Florida and settled down there with Roy. They would live there for a few years and then move to Tennessee and live there before getting a divorce. After her divorce, she moved in with us in Taylor.

Even that didn't mark the lowest point in my life at the time. That happened when my natural father showed up at my school.

CHAPTER 6

I was in first grade when Dad walked into my school. To say the least, I was confused. I didn't even know what he looked like. I was sitting in class when a messenger came to take me to the office. I didn't realize it at this time, but this was the first of several treks I'd make to the principal's office in the coming year. By far, this one would be the most pleasant.

I first thought something had happened at home with a brother or my mom. Instead, the principal asked me if I wanted to see my father. Of course, I said yes. I was taken into a small room and left to wait until my father came in. The door opened, and he stepped inside. Clarence Edward Pickle. He was a big man. I had not seen him since the night he threw a brick through our front window. Of course, it was dark then. I certainly didn't recognize him at school from that brief glimpse.

He sat down at the table and looked at me. There was a nice smile on his face. At first, I didn't know what to say. I had so many questions. My father said that he would do the talking. He said that he had a lot of explaining to do and knew I was nervous. He asked me how I was doing. I said

okay. He asked me if the school had told me who he was. I said yes; they said you were my father. He said that he loved me. He told me he always would love me and that I was his first-born son. I listened, building up my courage. Finally, I asked him why he waited so long to see me.

He answered me in a quivering voice. I saw tears form around his eyes. He said that my mother was keeping me away from him. He said that she threatened to call the police if he visited me at home. However, she told him he could see me at the school once in a while. He had agreed to that limitation. I asked him will he get in trouble for seeing me here in school. My father said he wouldn't, that he had parental rights.

He said there were laws allowing him to see me there. Naturally, I had more questions. I just couldn't ask them.

My father said I was tall for my age and turning into a good-looking young man. He asked me again how I was doing in school. We really didn't have much else to talk about. He didn't know what to say; I didn't know how to ask questions. I wanted to tell him how I was being treated at home, but, somehow, there just wasn't enough time. He told me to behave, be good for my mother and do well in school. I didn't bother to ask him if he was going to see David. I just figured he did. Later, after I went home, I listened to hear if David said anything about our father. He never did. I don't think my father ever saw him. He just came to see me.

I went straight home from school that day. We lived close enough that both David and I could walk home when Mom couldn't leave work to pick us up. I liked walking home. It made me feel grown up, but had a drawback. I had to walk with David.

My father's visit created a ruckus. After we had eaten dinner, my mother started yelling at me because my father had shown up at

school. I assumed the school called her and told her my father had come by. I didn't think anyone knew that he did because I had already been home from school for hours, and nobody had said anything about my father. Perhaps, she was thinking about what happened, too, just like me.

I remember my mother telling me not to ever mention his name. I guess she was thinking that I was going to tell her that he showed up at the school to see me.

I had been too afraid to raise the subject because I thought then she would take him away from me. All I could do that night was think about my father and how I looked so much like him.

My mother didn't do anything, but yell. Worse would come much later – after I made my second visit to the principal's office. I could have used my dad then. The problem started simply enough. Since John Haddock and Joe Brady were in my class most of the time, we would always play together. I started noticing around the end of first grade when we used to go to the playground during recess, that other kids, including John, started making fun of me because of my last name: Pickle. I didn't know why they were doing this. None of my neighborhood friends had ever made fun of me because of my name. The abuse would get worse over the year. Pickle isn't the greatest name, but it was my father's last name. I was proud to carry it.

In second grade, John continued making fun of my last name during recess along with some of the other kids. He just kept picking on me. One day, I had had enough. I knew it was wrong to get in a fight with him because I would get into trouble. I didn't want to be known as a tattle tale; kids despise that. Adults and the law call it a nark. No one wants to be known as a nark. You can get killed for that. I knew no better. Today, I would tell someone what was going

on, a teacher or the police. They are here to protect you. Neverthe-less, I was determined to make sure he never made fun of me again. Once one kid starts making fun of you, they all think they can.

John was in my gym class, and he naturally began making fun of my name again. "Hey, dill pickle," he sneered, "pick a peck of pickled peppers." There were other comments that were far worse. I won't mention them. I'd rather forget them.

He started pushing me repeatedly, acting as though he wanted to hit me. When he pushed me for about the fourth time, I proceeded to knock the crap out of him. I got him down on the floor and was swinging away at him, saying he will not make fun of me ever again. My heart was beating so fast that I was scared, but I just kept swing-ing until the teacher pulled me off him.

I knew I was in trouble, but, then again, John was not likely to make fun of me anymore. I had to put an end to it, so I did. Of course, John and I were sent to the principal's office. I knew the way very well by then. We sat until the principal came in. John had a bloody nose. His face was badly bruised. I had no idea what the principal was going to do to us for fighting, but found out soon enough. We were both expelled for a week.

The principal also called both of our parents. I remember going home after school that day and finding the doors locked on the house. My mother was home. All she would say to me through the window was that I wasn't allowed there while she was working.

Eventually, she let me in. I got whipped thoroughly. This was not as bad as what happened to me later. However, this is when she introduced me to the coffee pot cord. We had a coffee pot that Mom used in the morning. You had to plug it in, but its cord could be detached. Mom found a new use for it. She repeatedly whipped me

with that coffee cord. I ran from her to my bedroom as she was swinging the cord. I begged her to stop, but she didn't listen then or later. I jumped on my bed and grabbed my pillow for protection. She was yelling at me at the same time. I kept asking her to stop, but was hit with the coffee cord so much and was crying so hard before she finally did.

She left me locked in my bedroom like Ann always did. I was crying so hard that I didn't bother looking at myself or my body. I cried myself to sleep. After I woke up later that night, I was still locked in my room. I looked at my arms and legs.

I couldn't see my back. All I could see were big, black-and-blue, red welts. I looked like I had a just been flogged by a pirate on a pirate ship.

Everyday that she had to go somewhere during the time that I was suspended from school, my mother would tell me to get out of the house. I would be locked out of the house. That's how I learned to wiggle back inside. I had no food, no way to shower or change clothes unless I did.

Unfortunately, although I didn't know it at the time, my life would only get worse. I just knew I didn't want to be hit by that coffee cord again. I tried to avoid trouble, but it didn't take much to get my mother mad at me. She would always reach for the coffee cord. It must have been easier for her to hit me with the cord than to hit me with a stick or spank me with her hand. I knew this wasn't right, but what could I do? Ask my father for help? She would have only hit me harder.

I had a week to recover and hoped that these marks didn't become scars. Maybe people wouldn't notice them. I didn't do anything all week, but stay away from my friends. Somehow, the neighbors did

find out and started spreading rumors that I was being beaten in the house. All I ever figured out was that they must have heard me screaming through the window as my mother beat me with the coffee cord.

When I was allowed back to school, I immediately wore another path to the principal's office. He had set up a meeting with John, me and our teacher, Mrs. Ford, to find out what had happened between us.

John was in my class with Mrs. Ford, but I told the principal that I can't be in the same class with this kid as all he did was make fun of me. I told him why the fight happened, and that John had started pushing me and wouldn't stop. In fact, even after we went back to school, he started again. I said that I asked him repeatedly to stop, but he wouldn't. I admitted I shouldn't have hit him, that I was wrong.

I should have told the teacher or someone in authority. However, I said, all the other kids were starting to make fun of me, too.

All John could say was that I started the fight. He insisted he never called me names. However, to my surprise, the principal and my teacher contradicted him. They said they had talked to some of the other kids who were in gym class that day who agreed that he was making fun of me. John said that they were lying.

The principal decided I would stay in Mrs. Ford's class, but John would be moved. He went on to bully other kids and make fun of them, but he never bothered me again. Occasionally, since we were in the same grade, he would be near me, but he wouldn't make fun of me. No other kids made fun of me either. Instead, I became something of a magnet for kids being picked on. They would talk to me, perhaps hoping I'd in interfere with their tormentor, but I would

send them to tell their teacher. There was no way I was going to get into another fight.

David tried to make me break that resolve. He told me he was being picked on by someone I'll call Jeff. I was not surprised my brother was having a problem at school. After all, we had the same last name. David asked me to tell Jeff to leave him alone. David thought I was now a tough guy, but I really wasn't. Actually, I quickly realized that David just wanted me to get in trouble. Thanks to him, Jeff and his friends wanted to kick my butt and followed me around, waiting for me to start swinging. I wouldn't.

Instead, I knew my only chance was self-defense. I had no plans to ever fight again, despite my brother.

Jeff and his friends finally created a confrontation two years later. I was doing pretty well in fourth grade. While I was walking home from school one day, Jeff and two of his buddies followed me.

They kept yelling for me while I kept walking faster until they ran up and cornered me by the park on the corner of Huron just down the street from our house. There was a really big ice rink there. I remember we were on the hill near ice rink. I was so scared that I didn't even notice if anybody was ice skating nearby.

I thought they were going to beat me up. The three of them began pushing me around. I didn't know what I was going to do. They're trying to get me to fight them, but the odds were not good. Moreover, I didn't want to talk to my mother when I straggled home with torn clothing and a battered face. I didn't want any more trouble.

Then, I heard two girls who were ice skating. They yelled for Jeff to stop and to leave me alone. They even came over to help. I could not believe these girls were sticking up for me and standing up to Jeff

and his friends. It was Karen and Michelle. They knew the boys wouldn't hit them. We were all brought up back then never to hit girls. Actually, I thought the girls were going to beat them up.

Jeff and his friends ended up leaving. I thanked Karen and Michelle. Now you know why they remained my friends for years. In fact, this was when I started hanging around girls. They were much nicer than boys, never got in fights, better spoken and just plain pretty. After that, when we picked sides for sports, I would always be sure to get Karen and Michelle on my team. They were very good at sports, too.

I avoided that fight and another beating from Mom, but I couldn't get away from David that easily. I did fight with him. David would get me so mad, I would forget about focusing on defense. Unhappily, he would go crying to Mom. I would get whipped with the coffee cord and locked in my room again. He got away with everything, and I would fall right into his trap. David was good at that kind of thing.

Although simmering animosities cooled at school, my visits to the principal's office were not over. Soon after, I was invited back and taken to see the school counselor. My mother was there. The counselor wondered what was going on in my classes. He said I seemed normal, but was just getting by in school and didn't know why. He wondered if there might be something wrong with me since I had a problem with being able to pay attention in class. He thought I might have something he called attention deficit disorder (ADD). That was a new idea then. So, the counselor and my mother had set up an appointment for me to see a psychologist and to take some tests.

I had no choice. I was told I had to take those tests, and to talk to the psychologist about some of the problems I was having in school

and at home. A couple weeks later, once again, I trudged back to the principal's office. No wonder I couldn't pay attention. I kept waiting for the summons to the office. I ended up in the counselor's office where the psychologist was waiting.

He was a pleasant-looking man who had all sorts of papers on the desk in front of him and talked in a quiet voice. He asked how I was doing in school and if I thought I was doing fine. He asked me if I was having problems at home. I didn't dare tell him what was really going on at home. I was too afraid Mom would find out if I said anything and I would get whipped with the coffee cord again. I just said things were okay.

Then he proceeded to ask me a bunch of questions. After that, he gave me a multiple-choice questionnaire with a few hundred questions. I had to put a check next to the correct answer. He left the room leaving me alone while I did this.

Then he showed me some puzzles and stuff like that, and asked me to put them together as best as I could. I enjoyed that game. He said I did a great job. Then, he showed me inkblot pictures, asked me to look at them and tell him what I saw. What do they look like to me or resemble, he asked. So, I did. Afterwards, he said again that I did a good job. I have no idea what a bad job would have been.

We went over the inkblots again. This time, he wanted me to explain my answers: why did it look like whatever I said it did. I remember one that resembled a butterfly. He asked me to point out the aspects that made me think of a butterfly. We went through 20 or 30 before he decided I had done another good job. Then, I was asked to go back to class.

I never heard anything from him again. I figured everything was fine, and I was fine. There was nothing wrong with me. Actually, I

knew that. The problem was my mother. I should've told him what was going on at home.

I would see my father a few more times at school over the years, but, after that, I never saw him again. Eventually I learned, much later my father died, at the age of 32, after undergoing several heart surgeries, I was only 10 yrs old.

CHAPTER 7

After my near-fatal beating, I learned why my mother behaved so terribly toward me. All my aunts agreed that when my mother saw me, she saw my father. We looked so much alike. Aunt Lucy said that scared my mom, especially when I was mad or upset. Then, I looked exactly like him, she said. Her comments made sense. Eventually, all my aunts told me the same thing.

Unfortunately, the knowledge wasn't much help. My mom was beating me and taking out her aggression against her ex-husband because I looked like him. She needed help. No wonder when I mentioned my dad's name and said I want to live with him, she whipped me. She became another person.

The emotional turmoil naturally affected school. Throughout elementary school, I was just an average student. I passed, but without any distinction. I simply couldn't concentrate. Fortunately, there were a couple of teachers who touched me deeply and inspired me. One of them was my third grade teacher, Mrs. Ross. I'll never forget this African-American woman who was one of the best teachers I would ever have.

She spent a lot of time teaching me one-on-one, talking to me in a soft, gentle voice. I was always thinking about having a colored lady teaching me. I felt for her as I knew a little bit about slavery. Naturally, as a little boy, my sense of time was off since slavery had ended more than 100 years earlier, but I didn't realize that. I kept wondering how she ever got to teach. She truly was a motivational teacher. She understood me and what it took to motivate me; this inspired me to do well. I knew if she was able to go through the tough times because of her color and achieve her dream, teaching, then I could accomplish anything I set my mind to. I had the utmost respect for her. She was also the only black woman that I would ever come across in the teaching field for years to come.

One funny thing happened during the summer. We heard more about Evil Knievel, a stunt rider whose son, Robbie, is still an active daredevil. Evil died in 2007, which was a surprise. Considering the things he did, you'd have thought he would have been dead years before that. We followed Evil Knievel's career closely, thinking that this guy was doing death-defying feats and still alive. He became a phenomenon. Everybody I knew was paying attention whenever he did something outlandish.

In 1967, we heard that he was going to be on television, riding a motorcycle and jumping 151 feet across the fountains at Caesars Palace in Las Vegas. He ended up crashing December 31, 1967. However, his failure didn't detract from his legend, which spawned what I called the Evil Knievel days. Everybody in our neighborhood started setting up the bicycle ramps and seeing how far they could jump. I guess kids all over the country were doing the same thing. Eventually, he inspired an entire sport, which anyone can watch today during the X Games.

David was so infatuated with the whole thing that he almost turned into a miniature Evil Knievel. We started calling him David Knievel. He started jumping off garages. His interest didn't fade. As a teen, David bought a motorcycle and continued with the stunts. He didn't get hurt either.

As for me, I was more focused on girls. We were all thinking about girls: how pretty they were and what they were all about. My friends and I were fascinated with girls and a little girl crazy. I really didn't hang around boys at school anymore. Instead, I would just talk to the girls. Boys just tried to get me in trouble so I would just ignore most of them except my friends.

School took second place to girls. We were always thinking about them. Our bodies were changing. Every good-looking girl grabbed our attention. We really didn't understand why, but we wanted to talk to them, to get closer to them. All of my friends felt the same way.

I also found something else that was almost as enticing. At the end of the block was a park with a baseball diamond. One day, Mike, Chris, Eric and I walked down the end of the park and saw some kids practicing baseball. They were being coached by a short, husky man with red hair. We started asking him questions about how we could play baseball, too. We were afraid we were too late to sign up. The coach, whose name was Bob Lyle, said we weren't and that we could sign up at our elementary school. Mr. Lyle said he needed one more player on his team.

My friends ran home to get permission from their parents to play. I couldn't do that. I knew I needed permission, but I was too scared to go ask my mom. She never did anything for me, but I really wanted to play. I asked Mr. Lyle to talk to my mother. He came over the next day and even had the papers for her to fill out. He must have known I needed help.

My mom asked how much it would cost. Mr. Lyle turned and looked at me. All I could think is that I had no money. I didn't think my mom had any money either. Mr. Lyle replied that there was a $35 sign-up fee and $100 for the uniform. If we wanted to purchase the uniform through him, the shirt was free, but the rest of the clothes were not.

I started to walk away. I couldn't pay that. I knew my mother wouldn't. I must have had the saddest look on my face. Mr. Lyle stopped me. He said he would pay for the uniform and sign-up fee if it was all right with my mother. It certainly was. I felt like Mr. Lyle was taking a chance on me. I was determined to be the best baseball player for him.

I just couldn't believe how kind he was. I was also happy I could get away from my house and my mother for a long time. I ate and slept baseball all summer.

Mr. Lyle's two sons, Rob and Bob, played on the team, too. They had the same red hair as their dad.

The team was called Richmond. I was able to play right away because I was older. Being held back in kindergarten had actually been a help in this case. Richmond was part of Little League, but in the minors. I played on the team for three years and became very good. I would eventually be drafted to the Major Leagues. I used to pitch and play first base. I was an awesome pitcher, but I was tall, so, as a first baseman, I could reach far to get errant throws.

I always hated when a game or practice ended. Most of the time, the door to my house would be locked. I couldn't even get in the house. I would have to resort to taking a shower with the hose and started leaving soap outside to clean up. I started sleeping in a lawn chair in the backyard unless I managed to crawl through the base-

ment window. Even then, Mom usually locked the doors into the house.

Baseball taught me to be competitive, to be the best at something I really wanted to do. I decided I wanted to become a professional baseball player. I was 9 years old at the time. I never missed a practice or a game. Practices were usually on the weekends and consisted of batting, fielding and running, as well as an occasional scrimmage game against another team. This schedule would get more grueling as competition became better and the will to win was stronger. That first summer, we finished in second place and were in the playoffs where the two best teams played each other. The winners would get trophies. We lost, but I couldn't wait for the next season.

I almost didn't make it.

Every fall, my grandmother would come over to do some high-pressure canning. This would involve a big pressure cooker, lots of jars and pressure-sealed lids with rings. The process began by boiling water in the pressure cooker. Separately, we would place whatever fruit or vegetable we were canning inside a jar. The jar was then sealed tightly. We had to make sure the rubber on the bottom of the seal fit snugly around the rim of the jar. After the water reached the boiling point in the pressure cooker, we carefully placed the glass jars inside the boiling water. We could even stack the jars on top of each other as long as there was enough water inside the pressure cooker. Then the batch was cooked.

While my mom and grandmother were canning, I would sit there and watch them. It was pretty interesting, like a science project or something. After a batch was done, they would remove the pressure cooker from the stove and bring it over to the sink. They would then

take some steel tongs and remove each jar, placing beside the sink to cool. Then, they would repeat the process all over again.

One day, they were canning. I wanted to help them can. David was there to watch. My mom was trying to get the canning completed. I asked her how I could help. There was a batch of canned tomatoes just finishing up in the pressure cooker. She asked me to carry the pot to the sink after she had removed its lid. Then, I was to remove the jars and place them on the other side of the sink to cool down. She was going to put more jars back into the pressure cooker.

The pressure cooker was heavy. It was filled with boiling water and ten 32-oz. jars filled with vegetables. I had to be careful carrying the pot over to the sink. I didn't want to spill any boiling water on me. It was scary.

As I was carrying the pot over the sink, my brother came up behind me and deliberately pushed me. I end up dropping the pot. The boiling water spilled over my left foot.

He left quickly for a friend's house or went into hiding. I didn't see him for the rest of the day. I didn't care where he was. I was in so much pain and could barely walk. I kept going into the bathroom to run cold water over my foot in the bathtub. I would take some aspirin for the pain and go back to the kitchen. I told my mother that I probably should go to the hospital. My skin on my foot was blistering. The pain was awful. I showed her my badly swollen foot, but she couldn't take me to the hospital until the next day. By then, my foot was the size of a football.

I couldn't stand or walk on my left foot at all. I could only hop on my right foot to get to the car.

When we showed up at the hospital, a nurse brought out a wheelchair. The doctor asked how did this happen? I told him. The doctor

said I should have been brought in when it happened, not a day later. He said I had sustained a third degree burn down to the bone. He also said I would not be walking on my foot for at least three months. He said I wouldn't be able to play baseball for at least six months. In a way, that was okay since it was now fall. I had to be ready for next season Every time I would run, the force generated would be far too painful.

Just standing and walking on my foot was going to take a lot of physical therapy, he said. I had no skin, flesh or muscle in my foot. "It has been burned away."

The doctor prescribed a medicated ointment that I had to apply to my foot twice a day. I also had to see him to remove dead skin and to make sure my foot didn't become infected or catch gangrene. I could lose my foot. The doctors had to keep it wrapped in gauze.

I was told to keep my foot dry and elevated. I had to wash it twice a day with antibacterial soap and soak my foot in Epsom salts twice a day: once in the morning before school; and once at night before I went to bed. The doctor gave me crutches so I could walk around school and get around to my classes

I had to learn not only how to walk again with my left foot, but also to run. That caused excruciating pain, but I had to do it. I never thought I would get through it. The pain lingered so long that I thought it would never go away. I didn't think I would make it for spring training in March. I needed months to learn how to run again. Every time my foot hit the ground, a shooting pain traveled through my leg to my neck. It would knock the wind out of me. I almost give up until I noticed one thing. When I ran on the ball of my toes it didn't hurt as much. That style made me lighter on my feet, like a ballet dancer.

Of course, I didn't tell anyone I was dancing on my toes like a ballerina dancing.

The pain lasted for about a year. I learned a new style of running, which was actually faster than the old way. I could speed home faster than my friends and, I was stronger, too.

I could also play baseball when the season started again. We won the championship two years in a row. I was the deciding factor in one of the championship games. I threw a no-hitter in the championship game against the Yankees. My career as a professional baseball player was looking brighter

Baseball only took care of the summer months. I needed to do something during the winter that would keep me out of the house and away from my mother. Then, I realized that my next-door neighbors, Michael and his brother Tommy, were in Boy Scouts. To join, I had to sign up. There was that old bugaboo about my mother signing the forms, but Michael said any adult could sponsor me. That worked for me. I started going to Boy Scouts every week. Michael was not in my troop.

I would try to get a ride with one of the eight boys in my group. Most of the time, I couldn't. So, I would walk as long as the homes where meetings were held weren't more than a mile away. It was good exercise.

The most memorable time I had in Boy Scouts involved our soap box derby. This wasn't the national one held annually in Akron, Ohio, but it was just as important to me. A soap box derby car starts as a block of wood that is whittled into the shape of a car. You could make it look like anything you wanted. Then, you applied wheels to the box and weights underneath the car. Finally, you painted it whatever color you wanted. The object was to create the fastest car.

I had no experience and knew I needed help. My obvious choice was Uncle Charley, who was an engineer designer for Ford. He knew how to design a car. The problem was that he and Aunt Marion lived in Southgate, which was about 15 miles away. That was too far to walk, so I rode there on my bike.

Uncle Charley agreed to help. He would take the wood into work and mold it into a car. I had about eight weeks to get the car ready. When I went inside the house, I saw the car sitting on the counter. I thought it looked like a real Indianapolis 500 car.

I decided to paint the car yellow. I don't know why. I never really liked yellow on a car, but it turned out perfectly. Two weeks later, all the scouts, troop leaders and parents came to watch the race. There were hundreds of people at the track, which were long, wooden roller-coaster looking things about 50 feet long. They were divided into eight lanes; each lane had six tracks. There was room for 48 kids at a time.

Participants put their cars on the track. It was held in place by a piece of wood. The bar would go up, and the cars would roll to the bottom. The winner would be the one whose car arrived first. If your car won, you moved into the next heat. That continued until there were only eight cars left, including mine.

The first, second and third-place cars in the race would be the finalists. It was getting mighty loud in this gymnasium. I ended up second in the semifinal. Three of us would now compete for the title. My little yellow car was ready to roll. I said a little prayer and set up the car on the track. The other two boys also had their cars in place. I could feel the tension building. People stared at us. I could hear the steady hum of conversation.

Then, I heard the official running the race say, "go." The bar went off. The cars started down the slope. My little yellow car was in the lead, but a blue car was closing fast. The third car wasn't in sight. I clenched my fist and watched the two cars roll side-by-side. It seemed to take forever to reach the finish line. At the last instant, the blue car seemed to edge ahead and just poked its nose over the finish line before my car. I was so close that I wish they would have had a photo-finish camera there.

CHAPTER 8

Fifth grade brought Mr. Greenhill or, as we called him, Mr. Green Jeans. He would always wear these overall jeans to teach in. So, all the kids in class would call him Mr. Green Jeans. He actually seemed to like it. Maybe that's because a character on the popular Captain Kangaroo children's TV show had the same name.

He certainly wouldn't have made it on TV. The whole class thought he resembled a bug. Mr. Greenhill was tall and thin, but he had these big, bulging eyes that look like a dragonfly's eyes. They popped out from his face.

Mr. Green Jeans would teach me, and probably the whole school, more about insects, dinosaurs, or reptiles such as snakes and mammals and butterflies than any one person I've ever known in my life. To this day, I think this teacher was amazing. He had the biggest collection of insects. When it came time to study insects, reptiles, butterflies, and mammals, our classroom was like a museum. The whole classroom was a giant pin board. When it came time to study insects, he had just about every species there were. He told us what they were, what they've done and where they could be found and if they were related to another species. He had it all. The same with reptiles. When it came time to study them, he had every species of butterflies imaginable. It was just incredible. Mr. Greenhill spent

most of his life studying these creatures and collecting these specimens to share with his students.

I would have to say that Mr. Greenhill probably made the biggest impression on me compared with all of the other teachers that I have ever had.

I did very well in his class, but was introduced to something called corporal punishment. I knew all about it at home under a different name – abuse – but never heard of anything similar in the school before.

I guess we were old enough that, if we did not behave, teachers thought we should find out what corporal punishment was. We learned quickly that a couple of the teachers had paddles and used them to swat kids on the butt. Mr. Greenhill knew how to apply corporal punishment.

His main focus, of course, was on science, not swatting rear ends. However, he was an expert in both. I loved the class even though I got into trouble, sometimes for falling asleep and daydreaming about being famous and wealthy one day. However, what caused me the most pain was talking to girls. I continued to chat with Karen and Michelle along with a new girl from Greece. They made me feel good, and they were always nice to me. I think they liked me because I was never a threat to them. I didn't want to be their boyfriend and was too shy anyway. I was just their good friend, and I think the girls could relate to that.

When I talked too much in class, I got to meet Mr. Paddle. It was long and wide, and had holes drilled into it. That was to reduce friction. In the middle of Mr. Paddle, there was a marble. I still remember its color: blue. Mr. Greenhill was supposed to be the king of paddling. He would march me to a hallway, say bend over and whack. It sure did sting. I jumped around for a few minutes to cool off my can. You better not have gotten in trouble the same day twice or three times or you would get whacked three times. A couple of other kids did.

I tried not to get paddled. I also wanted to avoid getting into the amount of trouble one of my classmates did. Duane Charbonneau

and Mr. Paddle regularly got to know each other on a close, personal basis.

Duane was a strange person, really skinny and busy handing out candy to everyone so they would be friends. He was often paddled for coming back to school late after lunch. We would go to McDonald's, which was about eight blocks away for lunch.

We had to get back to class within an hour. Across the street was a party store. Duane would always stop and buy candy there, which usually delayed him enough to be tardy.

One day, I asked him where he got all this money to keep buying candy. He said he had a paper route. Then, I asked him why he gave those kids all his candy. He said that if he didn't, they would beat him up. This reminded me of my problems with John the previous year, so I told Duane to tell the teacher or go to the principal and tell him what was going on. He never did.

Then, one day, we found out he didn't have any money to go to the store. He went anyway and came back with a bunch of candy. It didn't take long for the school to realize he had stolen it. Later on, we learned that he was stealing money from his mother to purchase the candy. This time, Mr. Paddle wasn't needed. Duane was suspended. I never really knew what happened to him. I never saw him again. I looked him up recently on the internet and found a Duane Charbonneau who was an esteemed scientist, but I doubt he's the boy I knew. For starters, he wasn't studying candy.

I felt sorry for Duane because he felt the need to distribute candy to be accepted or liked by the kids at school. Although he was not my friend, he taught me a lot about compassion.

When classes ended for the summer, so did my career in elementary school. I would be in sixth grade next year at West Junior High. I hoped that meant a better life. Instead, I started having physical problems. We didn't have enough food at home, so I was filling up on candy bars. I couldn't take showers properly because I was forced to sleep outside. With puberty came another curse: acne.

My face was a mess. It was so embarrassing. My skin got so bad that I didn't want to go to school, but I did. David never had a problem with acne nor did George or John.

I really couldn't focus on baseball that summer. My team won the championship, which was great, but I was thinking more about how to get enough good food. To do that, I needed to make some money. There was no way I was going to get enough at home.

One day, I asked Mom if I could cut the grass. She said no at first. I told her that I had watched her and was sure I could do it. She thought I was being smart. I asked her to let me demonstrate. She cut part of the lawn, and then sat down and watched me finish. I must have done a good job. After that, I started cutting the lawn. I would cut our lawn once a week and then would go around asking the neighbors if they needed their lawn cut. I started making some money. Soon, neighbors wanted me to cut their lawns every week.

I started making $50 to $60 a week, getting paid $10 a week per lawn. I could afford to buy food. I just didn't know what to buy. I could only buy junk food. Of course, I had a problem. I wasn't allowed to use the stove. I could have purchased meat, but not have cooked it. These days, grocery stores have prepackaged meals, but that wasn't true then.

One solution was to time my visit to relatives' houses. Since I was older, I was walking or riding my bike farther. I would go over my Aunt Marion and Uncle Charley's house.

I really never tried to show up there for dinner, but, more often than not, they would always be eating dinner. I figured someone was guiding me to be there on time. After all, I never knew when they ate. The times varied. If my timing was good, they would always invite me to stay and eat over. That was always great, and I got to see my cousins Jerry and Sherry. For several years, it almost seemed normal to show up over there and spend time with my aunt and uncle.

I preferred to ride my bike since it took 45 minutes to get there, but David started to steal my bike when his broke. Then, I would walk.

I really needed to get away from the house. It was becoming even more crowded as Aunt Lucy and her boyfriend, Lee, set up house-keeping in our basement. We now had seven people in a three-bedroom house that was only about 800 sq. ft. and had one shower. With my Aunt and Uncle living in the basement, I couldn't crawl through the window at night. I would have to find other ways to get in the house or I would freeze to death in the winter.

I was able to sleep occasionally at a friend's house, but knew that wouldn't save me from the Michigan winter. I used some of my money to buy some nice clothes to start junior high while I tried to think of a solution. I still felt God's presence and still had faith that, one day, I would be rich with wealth and power so I wouldn't have to ever worry about a home or food to eat.

I saved enough money during the summer to buy a lawn mower from a friend. After cutting the grass one day, I was really dirty. So, I went to wash off with a hose. However, David turned off the water. He said he would turn it back on for a couple of dollars. I couldn't believe he was blackmailing me. Unbelievable. But, I had no choice. I said yes, and he turned on the water.

My mother drove up and saw me showering. She didn't ask why, but grabbed a 2 x 4 next to the garage and chased after me. She hit me across the back with it. I was in so much pain. The neighbors were outside and saw it all.

I ran over Mr. and Mrs. Sebastian's' house. Michael's older sisters, Karen and Kathy, were swimming in the pool in the back yard. They went and got me some ice. I had bruises all over me from being hit with a 2 x 4.

Michael said he'd ask his parents if I could stay with them. As we were walking outside, soon-to-be-uncle Lee pulled up and started yelling at me. He swore at me, told me to stay away or he'd kick my ass.

Lee was an alcoholic. From my limited experiences, people like that didn't know how to fight. He kept making threats. I tried to walk over and tell him what had happened. He said he didn't care. He then

tried to grab me and punch me. I backed away. He came at me again. As he grabbed me, I flipped him, throwing him over my head by using his momentum. He landed on the ground. I took hold of his neck and told him never to touch me again or I will beat the living shit out of him. I let him go and walked away. He wasn't moving. David and my mom had to come pick him up from the ground.

The neighbors standing on the porch saw what happened. I was just defending myself. I also I realized how strong I really had become. He was drunk, so it wasn't much of a battle, but I made my point. He never would lay a hand on me again or talk to me the way he did that night. And I never would talk to him again either.

Mr. and Mrs. Sebastian had seen everything. They asked me about other members of my family. That was a hard question to answer, and a very shameful and embarrassing question.

I could only answer this question one way: I knew my Aunt Marion and Uncle Charley cared about me, but they live too far away. No one else in the family seemed to care at all. I started to cry and said I really don't think they cared or they wouldn't let my mother treat me this way. They asked me to try talking to them, and I said okay, but didn't mean it. As embarrassed as I was and ashamed, I never would talk to my family.

In the end, I returned home. I had no place else to go.

At least, David got distracted by new neighbors. Mr. and Mrs. Carpenter across the street were moving. Their house would be vacant for a while, and then, in the fall, a new couple, Pat and Henry Hoover moved in. They had no kids and were in their mid- 30s. Pat was a fairly good-looking woman with long blonde hair; Henry was tall and skinny with long black hair with buck teeth. They seemed to have a lot of money.

David started spending time at their house. They used to stay up late at night, remodeling the home. Henry also worked on cars. They were up almost every night late, and I noticed David going over there all the time. He would be helping Pat and Henry do all sorts of stuff. Before long, he moved over there. He was only about 10 at that time.

Henry was a private person who didn't say much to other neighbors. In fact, Henry seemed really mean and always talked tough. He pretty much scared off all of us neighbor kids. But, for some reason, Pat and Henry liked David, probably because he was a great schmoozer. My mother just loved having David go over there to live. When school started, David would have the best of everything, especially nicer clothes than any of my friends had. Pat would always take him shopping for anything he wanted.

So, as time went on, David helped them remodel their house. Whatever work Henry needed to have done, David would do it.

Then, they had a daughter, Heather. David watched Heather whenever Pat and Henry went somewhere. As a result, none of us ever saw David anymore outside of school. When he went to classes, girls liked him. He would always be eating right and taking showers every day, but I couldn't do that. I was locked out of the house. George and John still wouldn't let me in. I would shower with the hose and soap in the backyard and sleep outside. If possible, I would sleep in the backseat of my mom's Ford Galaxy 500.

I always would remember sleeping in the car or on the front porch or on a lounge chair in the backyard on those hot summer nights. I would always hear a freight train going by in the middle of the night, blowing its whistle. I would listen to the sound of the locomotive engine clickety-clacking down the track as the years went by. It soon became soothing to listen to the train in the same way the ticking of the grandfather clock used to comfort me. Still, hearing the train made me feel so lonely. Even today, when I hear a train, it takes me back to those days.

CHAPTER 9

As summer faded, Michael again asked his mom and dad if I could move in with them. Michael knew I was ashamed and embarrassed to need a place to stay, but I had nowhere to go and would have to leave the area to survive. His parents said yes. I stayed at Michael's house for quite awhile, but started to feel embarrassed as if I were imposing on them.

Being over Michael's family's house with Mr. and Mrs. Sebastian's, I started to feel like a loser. Everybody knew I was living over there. I didn't know what to do if I didn't want to live there anymore. We got along and everything but there is just something else. I had to go. I just didn't feel like I fit in. I always wondered where I would fit in. I would finish up the school year, and I would have to leave. They knew I didn't know what to do, and they didn't know what to do either. I knew it really wasn't their responsibility.

Eric, another friend, said I could live in the basement of his house. Their mom had just gotten divorced, so she didn't mind. I shifted to Eric's house, but knew it wasn't my home. It was just a place to stay for the time being. I always asked myself when I was going to be kicked out. As a result, I never took off my coat, thinking I would have to leave at any time. My jacket was a comfort thing and made me feel secure. I never got over the uneasy feeling in someone

else's house. It took me years to overcome. During the next few years, I would live over different friends' houses around the neighborhood.

At least, I did well at West. My friends were all there. I remember one particular teacher who affected my life, Mr. Horvath. He was practically deaf and wore a hearing aid in each ear. Everybody would make fun of him, because they thought that he couldn't hear. However, students didn't know about volume control of a hearing aid. He heard everything. He also saw something different about me.

Many times, Mr. Horvath was asking me questions, but I didn't know what he said. This would go on for several weeks. Then, one day, he asked if I had had my hearing checked. Every year in school, we would all get checkups for hearing, vision, heart and blood pressure. I told him, yes; it was fine. He disagreed and said he would set up a meeting with the counselor. He thought I had a problem with my hearing.

He needed permission from my mother to send me to a specialist, but she agreed – to my surprise. It was the school's idea, not mine, so she went along. The doctor took a big scope and looked inside my ear. Then the nurse put me in a big room that looked like a bank vault. I didn't want to stay there, but the nurse said this was part of the test. I had to put headphones on and was tested all afternoon.

After the tests were done, the doctor reported that I had no hearing in my left ear. They didn't know why and ordered further tests a week later. First, they took x-rays of my head. Then, they brought out a tuning fork, which looks like a U-shaped piece of metal that you can hold in your hand. The doctor hit it, and it vibrated loudly against my right ear. It was so piercing that I pulled away. Then, he hit it next against my left ear. There was nothing. I didn't move.

That answered the question why I couldn't hear: I didn't have the nerve that vibrates to make sound. The eardrum was there, but, without the nerve, it might as well be collecting dust in an attic.

When sound waves strike the eardrum, it vibrates. The vibrations are transmitted through the middle ear by three tiny bones called

ossicles. The vibrations then pass to the cochlea in the inner ear, where they cause waves in the cochlear liquid. The nerve endings in the cochlear tube are sensitive to these waves. The waves then convert to messages that are carried by a special nerve, called the acoustic nerve, to the brain. Here they are identified as sounds. None of that happened in my head because I was born without an acoustic nerve.

Any surgery would have been too expensive. Besides, in those days, I doubt anyone could replace an acoustical nerve. I would have to listen with my right ear.

Many schools have the same ordinary hearing test, I was given just a set of headphones and a acoustical box for sounds. They do not detect a hearing problem. For many years, they found nothing wrong. You must be in a sound proof room where sounds waves are only directed to the right or left ear. Without sound openly traveling through the air, it's difficult to detect a problem.

The doctors suggested that I sit in front of the class on the left-hand side with my right ear facing towards the west side of the class. The move seemed to help. My grades went up to A's and B's. In English, I got A's on all the tests. I did very well in science and history, although I always found history boring. Most of the time, I simply tried to stay out of fights and get good grades.

As a side effect, my mother felt pretty badly that my hearing problem wasn't caught until I was 13 years old and started being a little nicer to me. Of course, I was also still living at friends' houses.

Every now and then, however, she would let me sleep in the house. I never could figure her out. Every time, I was sure she started feeling sorry for me, she would start locking me out again. I would still play baseball until late at night, practicing with some teammates and preparing for tryouts for the Major Leagues. Then I would come home and shower with the hose and a bar of soap. After which I would open up my Mom's 1965 Galaxy and sleep in the back seat.

CHAPTER 10

Seventh and eighth grade at West were complicated years, especially because of some of the new kids I met there. I had to contend with Ron King and the Shook twins, Ron and Bob. These guys always seemed to make fun of everybody in class and around school. They thought they were tough. I thought King was a burnout – a term we used for kids who dabbled with drugs. The Shook brothers were jocks. They liked to show off their muscles and play sports. They always wanted me to play football, but I was only interested in baseball.

I had to do my own thing. I think this intimidated some people, especially the burnouts and the jocks. They would follow me around, trying to pick a fight. Of course, they called me names because my last name. I just watched them, saw how stupid they were and learned from them.

Still, the pressure to conform was strong. Many kids were using pot, mescaline or acid, trying to fit in and be accepted. Everyone was drinking, too. I didn't. I couldn't afford to buy drugs or alcohol and refused to get involved with something like that anyway. I always

tried to be a leader, not a follower. Life was crazy enough at home without compounding the situation.

The pressure on me came to a head one sunny day at school. As usual, the Shooks were making fun of me and saying that they could kick my butt. Of course, David couldn't ignore that. My brother was such an instigator. He decided to tell Ron Shook, who was in my math class, that I could kick his butt. Nevertheless, I was determined not to fight in school. I had told myself I wouldn't, and I planned to stick to that vow.

Nevertheless, after school ended, Ron and I squared off. The whole school seemed to follow us to a field off school property. That way, we couldn't break school rules. While we walked there, I decided I was going to make an example out of Ron. If I lost, everybody would make fun of me. If I won, nobody at school would screw with me again.

I let him start. First, he pushed me. I let him hit me while yelling at him. "Come on," I sneered at him. "You hit like a little girl. Is that all you got?" I blocked blows to the face, but let him hit me in the arms and side. Slowly, I built up anger to let loose the beast in me. When I was ready, I swung at him and hit him on the left side of the face like he'd never been hit before. I threw lefts and rights as hard as I could. Then, I flung him to the ground and hit him some more. He stopped moving.

Then, his twin brother jumped me. I didn't care. One punch knocked him out cold. Ron slowly staggered to his feet, encouraged by all the kids around us shouting for him to start doing something. I looked at Ron and said, "If you still want to do this, you won't be walking home."

He stopped and gave me an odd look. "You're bleeding," I said. "Come and get me."

By this time, his brother recovered. In a moment, it was going to be two on one. They were tough guys, and I wasn't about to face them both at the same time. I went running at them and shouted, "You're done." They were. They quit immediately.

I wasn't proud of what I did. I don't like to beat up people, even when they deserve it. Still, I earned everybody's respect that day because I didn't back down: not because I wanted to, but because I had to. As a result, I was left alone at school. No one teased or made fun of me anymore.

The burnouts stopped calling me chicken because I refused to smoke pot, drink or hang out with them. On the other hand, girls started liking me more. I wouldn't have minded spending more time with them, but I never really had the time to.

For starters, I was back on the baseball diamond. I played pitcher and first base in the Major leagues on the Syracuse team against my friends Larry, Michael and Chris. Larry was on the New York Yankees. Michael played for the Dodgers. Chris played on the Blue Jays. So did Eric, but he quit soon after the season began. That was the first of four consecutive years I played for Syracuse. Each year became tougher and tougher playing baseball. No food, no home, keeping up with school, the homework: all of that was taking a toll on me.

Larry and I both became pretty good. We attracted some scouts who would come to the games to watch us. Our farm pro-league was then one step below the Major Leagues professional ball. Larry and I were both drafted to play in seniors. I played for the Houston Astros; Larry, the New York Yankees. We both dreamed of one day playing with the pros. I would sometimes drop by his home – just two houses from mine – so we would pitch to each other. Larry also had a batting cage at his

house to that we would practice hitting. He enjoyed martial arts, too. I found that very interesting and would soon take up on my own when I found the time. He taught me a lot of techniques.

At the same time, I continued to lift weights with Chris and Mike. We started going to Randy Samson's house for that. Randy was a very nice guy and shy, with a short, stocky build. He loved to compete in bodybuilding shows.

In the summer, several guys would join me in my backyard. Since we couldn't afford a real tent, we'd make one from blankets. We would throw a couple blankets over the clothesline that was hanging in the backyard pool and hold down the ends with bricks.

Then, we would put a blanket on the ground. With no parents around, we could just do about everything and anything we wanted. One time, Eric brought some beer. He probably got it from his older brother, Carl, who had a drinking problem. We also smoked cigarettes. Eric started that, too. I didn't know what the attraction was. Besides, I didn't have any money to buy cigarettes or beer.

If we got hungry, we'd walk over to Dunkin Donuts, which was about 10 blocks away from the house. We'd buy hot chocolate and a dozen donuts. Every night seemed to be a party.

One of the times we camped out, Chris mentioned David, my brother, who had gone to Canada with Chris and his parents the previous summer. Chris said David were always complaining that he wanted to get back to the Hoover's house. He then told us that David and Pat Hoover were having sex. At first, we thought Chris was just drunk. After all, David was younger than I was. Later, when I thought more, it made sense. Every morning, Pat would always open up her drapes at her picture window in a see-through gown. You could see her panties, and

she wasn't wearing a bra. I became so interested that, every morning, I looked forward to her opening up those drapes.

Still, we were skeptical until David joined us one night. He admitted he was having sex with Pat every day while Henry was at work. No one was going to say anything. Henry would probably shoot anyone who told him such a thing. He probably would have shot David, too.

I also got a shock at home. My mother started to act nicely toward me. It may have been a coincidence, but cops were starting to move onto our street. One, Joe Stephens, became our next door neighbor.

Another, Mr. Siebert, was another two houses down. He would eventually become the commander of the Police Department, a step below chief of police. A third cop, John Castle, lived on the next block.

Joe Stephens eventually talked to my mother about the way I was being treated. But, he and his wife soon divorced, and he moved away. Mr. Siebert couldn't really do anything either.

Fortunately, I was older and too big for my mother to hit me now. I wouldn't have struck her back. On the other hand, she was probably afraid that I would. She knew I could seriously hurt her if did.

Nevertheless, I still didn't get into the house very often. Occasionally, I could sneak into the basement if my aunt and uncle were away. Most of the time, however, I was locked out and would end up staying over one of my friend's house.

Things were not perfect: my acne got worse. I was eating a lot of greasy food at Pizza King along with candy bars, potato chips, soda and cookies. My acne spread to my chest and back. I was starting to

feel embarrassed around people. The acne was so bad that people were calling me pizza face. It was very hard for me to keep going to school and working while looking like a monster. My mom wouldn't take me to a dermatologist.

My focus, however, was on earning enough money to get my own apartment. Once, I went over Uncle Charley's house before school resumed in the fall. He asked me if I wanted to go on a moving job. I was delighted to make some money. He used to move furniture with his pickup truck to make extra money. That day, he was moving a piano into a house. He wasn't sure I was strong enough, but needed the help to pick it up and deliver it.

The first part was easy: we picked up the piano and put it inside his truck. Then, we took the piano to the woman's apartment, carried through the front door and were confronted by stairs. The apartment wasn't on the first floor. My uncle said we could do it one step at a time. We did just that all the way up to the top of the stairs. I couldn't believe we did it.

I got paid $60. My uncle asked if I wanted more work. Sure. It was easier than cutting grass and took a lot less time.

That summer before eighth grade was the best yet. Aunt Lisa and Uncle Todd got married and moved out of my house. Unfortunately, considering how Uncle Todd and I got along, their new house was on the next block. My brothers were now all in school. John started kindergarten; George was in first grade at Blair Moody. David was still living over Pat and Henry's across the street, which kept him out of my hair. Later, in October around my birthday, Aunt Marion and Uncle Charley added another boy, Andy, to their family. His brother Jerry was 8, then; his sister, Sherry, was 7.

Things got even better. My friend, Chris, found a job at Pizza King and said the owner, Jim, was looking for more help. Now, you can get a pizza delivered, but in 1972, few places did that. So, pizza parlors were popular places to hang out and watch chefs twirl dough in the air. Chris spoke to Jim on my behalf. Jim asked me to stop by. Pizza King was eight blocks from my house, about a quarter of a mile. I had to walk because I had outgrown my bike and needed a new one.

Jim was a big guy who looked like a football player combined with a hippie with long black hair and a beard. Because of my age, I could only work part time or four hours a day, no more than 20 hours a week. I also needed a workers' permit. I told Jim I could work after school as long as the job didn't interfere with baseball. He didn't see that as a problem.

Getting the work permit was easy. I got the forms at school and didn't need my mother's permission. I then went back to see Jim. He wanted me to work late nights and weekends, from 9 p.m. to around 2 a.m. I was concerned I might be a little late occasionally because of baseball, but Jim said he'd work around that, too. I had a job at minimum wage: $5.25. The next Monday, I started learning how to make pizzas.

That Friday, 9 p.m. sharp, after a week's training, I started making pizzas for customers. It was hectic. We closed at 2, but it took another hour to clean the place. When I got home, it was hard to take a shower with a hose when it was so cold outside. If I hadn't left the window open to get in the house, I would have had to sleep outside in the car

I got my first paycheck two weeks later — $105. That was a lot of money, but I needed more if I were going to have my own place to

live. I was making more money cutting lawns, but that wasn't much good in the winter with snow on the ground. I decided to see about delivering the Detroit News. These days, newspapers typically are flung from passing cars by anonymous adults. Years ago, however, a lot of kids got started in their careers by delivering newspapers. The Detroit News was an afternoon paper, another dying breed.

I went over to the Detroit News building in Allen Park and talked to a man named Steve. He said he'd get back to me. Later, Steve called to tell me that I could split a route with a young man named John Bailey. I called John. We met at Dunkin' Donuts at 3 o'clock in the morning and had a hot chocolate and a donut. We did this until I was trained to know the route. John became a friend. Even after I learned the route, we would still have our hot chocolate and donuts in the morning at Dunkin' Donuts before delivering the papers on the weekends.

Unfortunately, I ended up spending all the money I had left from working at Pizza King on a new bike to be able to do my paper route. The route covered about eight blocks east and west and another six blocks north and south. I did the paper route after school, but realized quickly there was a problem. How was I supposed to play baseball if I had to do the paper route after school? Most of my games began around 5 o'clock, but there were six of the 18 games on the schedule that started at 4 o'clock, right when I was supposed to be placing newspapers on front steps.

After I thought about it for awhile, I wrote a letter to all my customers and stuck it in with their bills. I notified them that I was playing baseball and that I would be late with the paper the day I had a game or possibly miss that day. I didn't want to cause a problem and lose any tips. During the Christmas holiday, customers always

tipped their paperboys. I made $700 my first Christmas on my paper route. My customers would tip me $20, $50 and $100, all nicely slipped into a Christmas card. John made $3,000 in tips, but he had around 2,000 customers. I split the route with him, but he kept the larger share.

My uncle wanted more help with moving, too. I knew that, once summer arrived and I was no longer in school, I would have plenty of time to do all three jobs. David wasn't around, so he wasn't being a pain in the neck. Most of my friends had jobs now. Mike joined me at Pizza King along with Eric. Summer settled into an easy, if busy, routine: newspaper delivery, baseball, Pizza King and making tents in the backyard. We would still get together to play baseball in the streets and, usually three times a week, go over to Randy's house to lift weights.

I would occasionally visit Aunt Marion and Uncle Charley to talk with them and get some career advice. Of course, I would get invited to stay for dinner. I thought I would make it up to them this summer by helping Uncle Charley remove an old tree root that was left over from a big tree he taken down to put in an aboveground pool in for his three kids.

I was really busy, but I liked it. I knew I was making money and moving ahead.

CHAPTER 11

I never told my mom that I was sleeping in the car. I figured she would start to lock the door. On the other hand, I did cause the battery to run down. She never did figure out that I was responsible for that.

My focus was on baseball and school. I was told by one of the scouts I had a chance to play for the Houston Astros' organization. There would be tryouts. The senior league was just below the professional farm system. Practices where more intense and grueling. Every other day, we ran three miles, with calisthenics, batting, pitching, and fielding; and scrimmage games twice a week lasting until the wee hours of the night.

One practice I remember fondly: a scrimmage game against the New York Yankees. I walked out to the mound to face my friend, Larry, and some of my classmates. Our league had some of the best players.

I seemed to have a following as we played on into the night. Girls and spectators chanted my name as I struck out a batter. This was becoming a trend when I played. I remember standing on the mound waiting for signals from the catcher, Joe, facing Larry at the plate. At

the end of the game, we won 8-6. The girls and the spectators were the highlight of the night for me. Exhausted and hungry, I walked a few miles back to mom's house.

I opened the car door, crawled in and went to sleep. I was so tired, I missed school the next morning. Mom caught me in the car. That didn't go over too well, she changed the knobs on top of the locks so I couldn't open the door with a coat hanger.

I was starting ninth grade and set a goal of achieving a 3.5 GPA, even though I took algebra, biology, English grammar and astronomy along with history, art and drawing. Naturally, I managed to get only a 3.0 GPA, but that was enough to move on to 10th grade.

I only got into one disagreement that year. Jeff, the older guy my brother had sicced me on a few years earlier, came up behind me and threatened me, pushing me again and again. After he left, I grabbed a shovel from the school maintenance shed. I came up behind Jeff and showed him the shovel. I agreed that he might kick my butt, but, afterwards, I promised, I would bust him with the shovel when he least expected it. One blow to his head, and, I said, I doubted he would trouble me anymore. I never heard or saw him again. His graduation was one reason, but I suspect my little metallic friend discouraged him, too.

After a year working the paper route and at Pizza King, I wanted to find something different for the summer and for after school. My friend Chris knew Gary Lumus, whose dad, John, and his uncle, Jack, owned D&L Garden Center. They cut lawns and did landscaping. A job with D & L paid $2 an hour more than the pizza parlor.

I eventually met with Jack, a tall guy who was very bossy. As we walked around the store, he busily issued orders to everyone in the store. He warned me the job was difficult, but I assured him I wasn't

afraid of hard work and promised I could work harder than anybody in this place. I got the job. I then gave my notice at Pizza King and at the newspaper. The following Monday, after school, I was on a D&L truck and was driven to a baseball field to lay sod. We had to lay thousands of yards of sod. It was hard and dirty work, but I didn't mind. I was getting stronger and making money. However, I had to stay up late at night to finish my schoolwork. The car light got quite a workout.

I started working weekends, too. Every Saturday morning, I would climb into a 24-foot flatbed truck with removable sides. By 8:00am, we were loading rolls of sod by hand. Each roll weighed about 80 pounds. Then, we headed to the baseball field. When we finished emptying one truck, another would show up stuffed with tons of sod.

I ended up laying sod for months during the week and on weekends. I would come home filthy from head to toe. I still took showers with the hose late at night. I would freeze my butt off, but I had to get cleaned up to be able to go to school in the morning.

If I wasn't at the garden store, I was helping Uncle Charley with his moving business. I didn't have to worry about David. He was with Pat and then dropped out of school after 10th grade.

One afternoon, my mother gave me a ride home from Uncle Charley's house. We stopped at a Christmas ornament store. After we went inside, I started to feel ill. I looked around, and my mother and her car were gone. I had to walk about five miles home through the rain and cold. By the time I arrived, I noticed my lip hurt. I thought that it could have been a toothache. I broke a window to get in the house that night to stay warm. When I woke up the next morning, my lip was swollen with what looked like a cold sore. My mother

shrugged off my complaint. The pain increased, and my face turned red.

My mother said she didn't have time to take me to the doctor. I couldn't go to school the next day. I looked horrible, and my mother locked me out of the house. I walked around all day. By the time I came home, my face was swollen. I looked like something out of a monster movie. Blisters covered the right side of my face and were spreading fast. I begged her to take me to the doctors. Fortunately, Aunt Lisa was visiting.

She took one look at me and told my mother to take me to Oakwood Hospital. I remember that I was in so much pain that I would black out at times.

After blood tests, the hospital physician, Dr. Kim, said I had a severe staph infection. He said if I wasn't hospitalized immediately, I would be dead in an hour. No one knew how it started: maybe a pimple got infected; or I cut myself shaving, although I don't remember cutting myself. However, my acne was so bad that I believe it got infected and turned into a staph infection.

I was placed in isolation for three weeks. Nobody could come to see me or was allowed near me. I received morphine three times a day to keep the pain away. It was like being hit in the head and face with a baseball bat. I wanted to die. I had IVs stuck in every part of my body: my elbows, my wrists, my hands, my toes. Anywhere nurses could stick an IV, they stuck it.

All I could do was pray. I couldn't even get up out of bed to go to the bathroom. Nurses gave me a sponge bath every day. They were so kind and compassionate. They would take alcohol with cotton balls and clean my face to try to dry up the blisters and oozing pus from my face. It burned a little bit, but it was helping dry up my face.

Dr. Kim would have me on a high protein diet. I could only eat certain foods. I can still remember one spinach dish that stunk up the whole room. To this day, I can't get that smell out of my head.

When my relatives heard I was in the hospital, they would call me on the phone and send get- well cards and flowers. Karen and Michelle from school sent me a card and flowers. All my neighborhood friends called and sent cards, too.

I'm glad they couldn't see me. My face looked like blown up tomato with scabs and blisters all over it. I ended up with scars not just from being abused, but also from the acne that spread across my chest and back.

My mom apologized and promised she wouldn't ever treat me the way she did ever again. She asked me to forgive her for the way she treated me. She asked me if we could have a fresh start. She kept telling me that she did love me and that she needed to get some help. She said she didn't know what she was doing. I told her I used to love her, but that she had beaten all the love that I ever had for her out of me. I was not afraid to talk to her that way, because I had no feelings for her and didn't believe a word she said to me. Look at me, I told her. I look like a monster now. She started crying

Finally, on Christmas Day, I was allowed to go home. Dr. Kim said that I would have to follow up with him over the next several months to make sure that all the poisons were out of my body and that my face dried up. He prescribed some pain medication and antibiotics that I would have to keep taking for several months.

When I walked into Aunt Cathy and Uncle Al's house, everybody greeted me warmly. I was so happy to be out of the hospital. A week later, school resumed. My face was still a little swollen with scabs all

over. I would have to use isopropyl alcohol three times a day to help my face dry up.

My mother was showing compassion. I believed she was trying to change. I tried to get along with her and forgive her for the past, but I couldn't forget. She did help me get my driver's license and a car.

For years, I saw another physician, Dr. Starrico, a renowned dermatologist, once a week. He gave me a shot of tetracycline in the arm and noted my progress. Then, I saw Dr. Starrico only once a month. My face, chest and back cleared up after about a year, but I was left with scars on my face from the staph infection.

It would take years for them to recede. I continued on the medication tetracycline, one of the most potent medications for acne, for years and still today have some scars. Today, there are stronger drugs for acne: the strongest being acutane.

Because of the timing, I didn't miss that much school. My first day back was kind of scary. People were staring at me and asked me what happened. I told them. I felt like a monster and was feeling ashamed of the way I looked. I also didn't have any nice clothes to wear to school.

Things got worse. I couldn't keep working at D&L Garden Center. I had to stay out of the sun to prevent sweating. Dr. Starrico said the sun would do well for my complexion and my body, and it would help dry up the acne. However, sweating in the sun and working around dirt was not a good combination. I certainly didn't want to take a chance on getting an infection again by laying sod

At least, at home, my mom seemed to be keeping her promise. I know she was trying.

While I was finding it hard to show up for school every day for several months, I still kept my faith in dreams. I always prayed to

God to show me the way, to give me strength and wisdom, and, most of all, protect me. I knew I was going to have to work hard for anything I would want to achieve in life. Praying and having faith is one thing. Work is another. You don't achieve success by doing nothing.

You must work hard, without any doubt, and have the faith to believe and know that, with passion and drive, you will succeed.

I learned that by watching Uncle Charley. I don't even think my aunt or uncle knew how much I would watch and listen to them. He showed me how to move furniture while we were on moving jobs together.

He also showed me the basic principles of a small business cash flow, pay scale and percentage of net and gross. He not only worked at his job with Ford Motor Company, but went to college at night to further his engineering degree. In addition, he put an addition on the back of his house, raised a garage to pour a new floor, remodeled his basement and much more. He also took care of his wife and their three children. That was a job. His faith and effort inspired me.

Just when everything seemed to be improving, my grandmother moved back into our house. I knew what was about to happen with my grandmother moving in. No matter what I did, it was my fault. The only solution I could see was to get a car and go far way. However, even with my mother willing to sign the papers, I still needed $350 for a Driver's Ed class. And, my mother wasn't going to cough up that kind of dough.

I had to borrow it. Doug, Chris's older brother, agreed to lend me the funds. I paid him back by returning to D&L. I worked there for a few weeks, made enough money and quit again. I just couldn't risk another infection. Soon after, I was driving my mom's burgundy

Ford Galaxy to the grocery store, to the mall or up to the gas station to fill the car up with gas. Mom was actually very nice and tried to teach me how to drive. She might have enjoyed the experience more if I hadn't made her panic while driving in traffic. Still, she took that risk, and I respect her for that.

She then bought a 1976 Ford LTD from one of the neighbors down the street. It had everything: power windows, power steering, power seats, rear defrost and automatic climate control. However, now that my mother had purchased this new car, she was more hesitant to allow me to drive it. Still, I did manage to get behind the wheel occasionally with my mom nervously perched next to me.

Soon after, my mother came home with a man named Chet. She said that he worked with her at Ford and that he was her foreman. He said that I probably wouldn't be old enough to work at Ford, but he would try to see what he could do. My mother didn't tell us that she was dating Chet. You just kind of figured it out when he began to show up at the house after work every night and then eventually started spending the night.

Chet didn't have much to admire. He talked like a southerner, wore a cowboy hat, had a bad complexion, no teeth, smoked and drank. He just looked like a bum and dressed like one.

It wouldn't be long until he and my grandmother were fighting. My mother would just listen to Chet. My grandmother finally moved out of the house and into Aunt Lisa and Uncle Todd house. I was thrilled.

My mother found out that Chet was an alcoholic, but she stayed with him and married him. I have no idea why. She threw out my father because he was abusive and an alcoholic.

I didn't like Chet at all, and he knew it. He liked guns. When he had a few too many drinks one day, he pulled out a gun on me and

David. I didn't really have much time to think; I just reacted. I ended up breaking his hand and wrist as I threw him to the ground. It would be the last time he tried to do that. Luckily, he was drunk. He probably would've been able to pull the trigger if he hadn't been.

David called the police. My mother got him out of jail, but the police pressed charges against him for attempted murder, assault and battery with a deadly weapon.

In response, a few days later, my mother threw me out on the street again. Although I got my driver's license, I didn't have a job or a car. I couldn't go back to work for the garden center because it was too dirty. I couldn't go back to work at Pizza King because the hours that I could work weren't available. I finally got a job at a gas station. The owner, Mark, trained me how to pump gas, collect from the customers and write them a receipt. That was back then. Now a days, it's "pump it yourself" in most states.

I had to ride my bike three miles to the station, but I didn't care. I had a job and some money. Now, I needed an apartment. At 16, I wasn't old enough to apply for an apartment by myself. I also didn't have any established credit. Since I had paid Doug back the money that he had loaned me, I asked him first about sharing an apartment. He had a girlfriend, Debbie, who wanted to move out so he would have more privacy. I also knew he wasn't happy living at home anyways with his brothers and sister. They were always fighting.

We would finally find a place at Southland Apartments on the south end of Taylor. Rent was about $650 a month. Doug and I became great friends as roommates. We would go out together to clubs. When his girlfriend would visit, he would let me take his car out for a spin.

I was still working at the gas station, helping my uncle move furniture and playing baseball for the Houston Astros in the Senior League. The only things I owned were the clothes on my back and a bed bought with some of the money that I had saved from work.

Unfortunately for me, Debbie and Doug started to think about marriage and having their own place. I was happy for them, but concerned about paying the rent. I didn't make enough money for that. Thankfully, I didn't need a car to go to school.

The school bus stopped in front of the apartment complex. I also started working 30 hours a week at the gas station. With Social Security money I received from my father, I was close to paying the bills.

Doug finally suggested I let my brother David move in. He had been kicked out of Pat and Henry's house. Apparently, Henry had caught them in bed. Henry got so mad that he pulled his 45 Magnum out of the closet, ready to kill David as he pointed the gun directly at his penis. Pat jumped up and down in the nude and screamed for her husband not to kill him. Henry finally told David to get dressed and get out. That's what David told my friend, Chris. Even stranger, David continued to go back to help around the house while Henry was working.

Although David obviously needed a place to live now, I thought having my brother as a roommate was a terrible idea. Doug insisted David had changed, but I was so sure that he had not. A few days later, Doug showed up with David, who was supposed to be getting a job at the Hyatt Regency hotel in Dearborn.

I said I needed time to think about it. I talked to Uncle Charley, who told me not to let David move in. On the other hand, I needed someone to pay half the rent. None of my friends could.

Doug did find my brother a job as a bartender at the Hyatt as promised. With that, I surrendered. David moved in. I hardly saw

him. I was determined to graduate. He was busy working. On the other hand, he didn't pay his half of the rent. I left a note on the table and asked him to leave the money for his portion of the rent, but he didn't.

Instead of going to work one day after school, I stayed home and waited for him. I told him he could go back to Pat and Henry's house or do whatever he wanted, but if he didn't pay his half of the rent by Friday he had to leave. I would change the locks so he couldn't get in the apartment anymore.

He didn't pay anything. So, I changed the locks. When he came back on Friday, pounding on the door to be let in, I had to threaten to call the police. He would eventually go somewhere: I didn't know where and really didn't care. Later, I learned David moved back in with Pat and Henry. I never did understand why Henry would ever let David come back and live with them. Maybe Henry liked the idea of Pat having sex with a minor. They moved soon after into another fixer-upper house. David removed all their big trees in the backyard, painted, remodeled the house and built a garage. I guess that's the price you pay to be able to have sex with the wife and a place to live.

Meanwhile, I realized I needed a car. Mom was thinking of selling her Ford LTD. I spoke to her about it, but she wouldn't give it to me and laughed when I offered to buy it. On the other hand, my grandfather was planning to get rid of his Chrysler Imperial, and she was thinking about buying it. The car was beautiful with crushed velvet interior seats and loaded all the bells and whistles.

He might give her the car or sell it to her for just a little bit. So, I kept hounding my mother about her car Maybe we could work out a deal for the car, I thought.

Meanwhile, I was riding my bike. It was January and cold. I finally got home around 12:30 a.m. to discover my brother had kicked in the apartment door. He also punched holes all over the wall and broke my refrigerator door off its hinges. Somebody from security came up and asked me what happened because there had been a complaint.

I guess a neighbor had heard my brother banging to get in the night I sent him away. As a result, I was evicted and given 30 days to move. I was also responsible for the damages. Fortunately for me, Doug's name was on the lease so his credit was affected, not mine.

However, I no longer had a home. My mother did finally give me her car after she got my grandfather's. However, I had no home. I couldn't sneak into my mother's house because Chet had a shotgun and threatened to use it.

To earn more money, I tried odd jobs. I sold paintings door to door at different businesses with my friend Carl. I just wasn't making enough money. I would make about $5-$10 for each painting that I sold, but I was using all the money just for gas for the car. I even tried to sell Kirby vacuum cleaners door to door. The first time, I demonstrated the vacuum cleaner was at my Aunt Marion and Uncle Charley's house. It was good practice. I would have made about $500 a vacuum, but nobody had any money. So, that didn't work.

My friends tried to help. Several times a week, when their parents weren't home, one of them would let me come over the house, take a shower and give me some food. Once in a while, on weekends, I would spend the night at their house. After a hectic year, however, I still was stuck sleeping in the car most of the time. The fact I now owned the car was no consolation.

CHAPTER 12

I survived the chilly Michigan winter thanks to having my car and some good friends, but still needed to find a place indoors. Unfortunately, I ended up hurting myself again. Eric and I stupidly walked through a park near his house late one Friday night. It was nice to feel the cool grass on my bare foot until I stepped on a broken beer bottle. A big piece sliced through my right foot. I pulled it out, but needed 18 stitches to close the wound. When the doctors finished sewing me up, I couldn't stand or walk on my foot for about three months.

That ended any chance of working that spring. I also missed a lot of classes and was five credits short of the twenty-one I needed to graduate. Hobbling on my crutches, I went into a school counselor's office and explained my situation. Could I take summer classes to be able to receive my high school diploma? Yes, I was told. I needed to pass math, biology, English and history. I would have to attend summer school every weekday during the summer for the next two months. Moreover, I would have to pay $365 for the privilege, and I didn't have that kind of money.

The counselor then mentioned the General Educational Development (GED) degree program, which was designed for dropouts and kids like me. To get my degree, I would have to pass tests in five areas: writing, social studies, science, reading and mathematics. Those tests cost only $180. I figured I might be able to come up with that sum if I sold the stereo in the trunk of my car along with some records and tapes and my 12-string Gibson acoustic guitar.

I was able to sell my guitar and stereo together for about $300. Then I started studying. I was still not eating right or sleeping very well in the car at night. I was growing too big to stretch out comfortably in the backseat. Nevertheless, I persevered without any family support. Nobody else seemed to care whether I graduated or not. However, I knew this was my future and that whatever happened was up to me.

Something inside provided the impetus.

In March, I drove downtown to the test center. I filled out a couple forms and was ushered into a large room. Maybe 300 other kids were already there. On the first day, I took three of the tests, starting with writing, then social studies and finally science. All of the tests had hundreds of questions. I was there seven hours with only a 30-minute break for lunch. I went home, parked the car in front of my mom's house and studied for the reading and math tests.

At 8 a.m., the next day, I was in that same room to be tested again. I wasn't sure how I did the first day, but felt better about my results on day 2. Of course, only the score mattered, not my feelings. I wouldn't find out the results for eight weeks. Just to reduce anxiety, I went to church on Sundays whenever I could and prayed to God that I would pass. Every day, I would wait by the mailbox at my mom's house. That was my only permanent address. No one was

going to deliver to a car. The rest of the time, I went from friend's to friend's house, taking showers and eating when I could. At least my foot healed in the interim.

Finally, the letter arrived. I was so anxious that I could barely open it. I nervously read down to the result. I had passed. I immediately called the testing center. The clerk checked and said that I had achieved some of the highest scores that that office had ever seen in years. The state Board of Education would issue the diploma in a few weeks.

For the next six weeks, I waited in front of my mom's house in the car every day for the mailman. I had to get the diploma and didn't trust what my mother would do if she got it first. Finally, July 18, 1980, I received my high school diploma and my GED. I was the first person in my family to graduate high school. It was one of my proudest days of my life. From that moment, I knew, whatever I put my mind to, I could achieve. I would never give up.

I was ready to prove to my family they were wrong about me. Now, I was on a mission. The sweetest revenge is becoming success-ful. First, I had to find a job. These days, kids can go on Craig's List or some other internet site to find work. Our only recourses in the 1980's were newspaper classified ads. I looked for something in landscaping, because I liked working outdoors. If that didn't work out, I had another option: furniture moving. Maybe I could start my own business doing that. I also planned to play baseball, hoping to reach the major leagues. That could be worth millions of dollars. I also wanted to go to college and take engineering and architect classes. I even considered becoming a pilot. I really felt opportunities were everywhere, now that I had my degree. Today, of course, everyone needs a college degree and probably two or three more. But, back then, a high school diploma really meant something.

However, I had to find a place to stay. I couldn't keep living out of my car like this. I definitely didn't want to live through another winter like the one I had just gone through.

I found an ad for tree trimming and tree removal. The ad said classes were forming now for Davy Tree Service and that the pay was good, but that I needed my own transportation. All of that sounded good to me.

I spoke to the company secretary, Sharon, and drove over the next day to fill out the application form. There were four spots still open in the class. I met the foreman, Mark, who later hired me. Meanwhile, I took empty bottles and cans to the store to earn gas money to drive back and forth every day to the training facility. I also borrowed money from Ricky, Chris and Doug's older brother.

Five days a week, I got up at 5:30 a.m. and drove the 45 minutes to Grosse Pointe. I learned everything from how to prune and trim trees to how to climb with climbing gear and "drop" a tree. We were taught about different tree diseases and how to treat them, and about different kinds insects that harmed trees much like a Horticulturalist. We also learned how to use heavy machinery to remove a stump.

I enjoyed it. My first paycheck was for $320 after taxes. That wasn't a lot of money for the amount of work I was doing. However, I stayed positive, knowing that the experience I was getting was worth more.

After paying off loans, I thought it would be nice to spend some of the cash on a graduation party. My friends had parties. It was a way to say goodbye, since all of us would be going in separate directions. If I didn't host my own, who in my family would? However, my mother refused to let me use her house even if I paid for it. I kept thinking of ways to have the party without her knowing. She did

leave occasional, either for a vacation with George and John, periodically to get away from Clifford or to take a couple of horses she owned to shows.

While scheming to use the house while everyone was away, I managed to relocate from my car. One Saturday, I worked overtime. When I stopped by my mother's house, I found a car in the driveway.

Two people met me at the front door. One was a very large, powerful man. I would later find out he won the tough man contest one year at Joe Louis Arena in Detroit. He was my dad's nephew, Ken. The woman with him was my father's mother. Strangely, my mother had let them into the house. Maybe Ken's size scared her.

My mother asked me talk to them. I told them about my job and that I was looking for a place to stay. Ken left me his phone number and told me to call if I needed help. I spent the night at Eric's house and then called Ken. He lived some eight blocks away. I drove over and met his wife, Rose, who was five months pregnant. They agreed to let me move in with them for a small monthly rent. I stayed out a lot to give them some privacy, but at least I was no longer living in my car.

Things picked up on the diamond, too. I was pitching one Saturday morning when a bunch of girls from my high school showed up. They just wouldn't stop yelling out my name during the game. I couldn't believe I still had a following. They said the game had been announced on the radio as well as the news I would be pitching.

It was very exciting. I wasn't dating then, not with the acne scars on my face. Besides, I had nothing to offer them. I didn't actually have a home. I was constantly working and had no money to wine and dine any of them. I was still pretty shy around girls. Little did I know , women would become my downfall. Only much later would one woman

become the ultimate source of strength in my life, one I would ultimately live for and love for the rest of my life. She was the gift that changed me forever, the angel who sat down beside me.

I just played baseball. I recall winning a game one day and felt like a stud having all those girls chant out my name in front of the other spectators. One of the girls, Teresa, kissed me. Everything would have been all right if she had stopped there. However, she asked me when my graduation party was.

That dovetailed nicely with what I had been thinking. I told her the party would be in a couple of weeks. She gave me her phone number and asked me to invite her. She said some of her girlfriends would come, too. Then, she kissed me again.

This was going to be my last game unless I found the time to practice and travel with the team. Each game was in a different city every week. That was impossible with my heavy work schedule, commuting daily 100 miles roundtrip to Gross Point, and staying with Ken and Rose. Finding my own way in life was difficult, at times very dark. Baseball was life itself to me the light that filled the void and gave me a reason to live. But when was I going to find the time to play?

As everyone left that last game on a hot and muggy evening, I sat on the bleachers A slight breeze filled the air. Overhead, the stars lit up the dark sky. Slowly tiring as the night went on and lying on the bleachers, gazing at the stars, I reminisced through my 10 years on the diamond and dreamed of the greatest game I could ever play.

The wind is calm, the grass is damp. As the lights lit up the field, the mood is tense, expectations high. We are playing against the New York Yankees for the championship. The game is being broadcast live throughout the country.

The National Anthem plays. The fans stand. Both teams line up in front of the dugout as the starting lineups are read. The crowd cheers.

"Play ball," the umpire yells.

Running out to the mound, I can feel the intensity building. We have the home field advantage and the last at bat. My team is behind me. I must lead them to victory.

Leading off for the Yankees is second basemen Kenny Sykes, who is batting 250.

I wait for the signal. I nod my head. I wind up, holding the ball tight in the palm of my hand concealed by my glove. I throw as hard as I could. I see it smack into Joe's glove. Strike one, the ump yells. Back on the mound, I talk to myself as the ball rolls in my hand. Joe is back in position. I wind up. I throw. Thud. Strike two. A curve ball right in the glove. Walking around the mound, I position myself, right foot on the rubber as I stare down the batter. I wipe the sweat off my brow. I shake my head, asking Joe for a different signal. I wind up and throw. The batter swings and misses.

Str—-ike three, the umpire bawls. You're out.

For the next eight innings, that's how the game went: striking out batter after batter. The opposing pitcher was at the top off his game that night. So was I. Neither team could score. Both of us were headed toward no-hitters. One team had to win. One was sure to lose, but the game did not climax until the ninth inning.

The fans are getting anxious, anticipating a win. The Dome erupts into a frenzy. Everyone in the crowd is on their feet. I run out to the mound.

Umpire yells, "Play ball."

Top of the ninth. Leading off for the Yankees, Jerry Stoles. I am standing on the mound, staring down at Stoles. Joe crouches down, adjusting his face mask. He pounds his glove with his right hand, saying, come on come on. He gives me the signal. I shake my head. No, he tries again. I finally nod as I wiped the sweat running down my face.

Gripping the ball as hard as I could, throwing a fastball down the middle. A smash to shortstop Ricky Moss. Moss throws over to first. Stoles is out.

The fans are chanting Astros, Astros, Astros. Only two more outs. The pressure is intense. My mind is focused, and my heart is pounding as my right foot touches the rubber in the center of the mound. Joe gives me the signal. I nod, staring down at the strike zone like I was going to burn a path straight to his glove.

My manager comes out to the mound. He tells me to settle down. I tell him I'm okay, nodding my head up and down. The bullpen gets busy anyway. Joe goes back behind the plate

Jack Connor is at the plate. Joe crouches down; the signal; I nod. I wind up, throwing a fastball. Connor swings and hits a towering drive to centerfield. Keck runs to the fence. He jumps up, catching the ball. I breathe a sigh of relief.

Two outs, one to go top of the 9th

The Yankees bring in power house Roy Johnson to pinch hit. I stretch, trying to stay loose. Johnson has a.300 average. He can hit.

As I stand there, with the fans chanting; the Dome, ringing; the pressure, immense. The noise is piercing. I focus, getting into my zone. The only person who stood between me and a no-hitter is Roy Johnson. I place my foot on the rubber, stare down at Joe. As the sweat rolls down my face, he gives me two signals. The second I

accept. My palms are sweaty. I step back. I pace as I psyche myself up. The hair stands up on my body; energy flows through me. It's time. I place my foot on the rubber. I wind up. I throw as hard as I can, a fastball straight down the middle.

Stri——-ke one, the ump yells.

Keeping the momentum going, I waste no time. I place my foot on the rubber. Joe gives me the signal. I accept. I wind up. I throw a curveball just slightly inside the plate. Stri——-ke two.

I walk around the mound. The crowd in a frenzy, chanting my name, giving me energy and power. This is for the championship: one more strike. This one is for the fans. My teammates smacking their gloves with their fists. Come on, Mike. You can do this. Without hesitation, I place my foot on the mound as Joe gives me the signal. I accept the first signal. I wind up giving it everything I've got. I throw a fastball inside and low.

Stri——-ke 3. You're out.

Yankees take the field. Larry Jones heads to the mound. Justin Lord pinch hits.

Lord swings. The ball rises majestically toward left field. Fans are on their feet. Lord stands by the plate watching. We jump to the front of the dugout. The ball is going down, going, going, gone. It's into the seats. The Dome is rocking, the ground shaking like a rocking volcano.

What a game. I did it.

Hearing a bell go off at the school, I wake up, dirty, sweaty and sore, walking home while scheming and plotting a graduation party I had to have, knowing that I would play no more. Baseball was a dream. Although I came close to achieving that dream back then, today, the game is a lesson learned.

Some dreams remain just that, if people don't act them out. They don't take initiative and mold the dream, and set goals to make it become a reality. Anything is possible, but you have to try or you will never know if you could have achieved that dream. I had choices and decisions to make. I made them with no regrets. Some dreams you abandon to go on to a bigger dream, setting your dreams higher each time. The love of baseball for me was my escape from reality, a way of acceptance, of feeling needed.

Baseball taught me discipline to be competitive, and how to win and lose gracefully, to have faith and never give up.

My will, my drive to overcome all odds, were formed there. For school, you just had to show up and learn. Baseball is a career. You play to earn a living, play for the love of the sport; you play to be the best at what you do: a "winner"

I had no backing, I had no support. I miss only the fans and the loud cheers.

I made it 10 years. Now, I was in control of my life. I had to earn to support myself. I could not wait for maybe or if, I would get drafted to the majors. That was a dream that had to be discarded. I had to make money now without baseball. I took control of my future

After giving up baseball, I learned never again to concentrate on a single profession or skill. Since then, I have developed, many skills and become diversified, eventually turning into an entrepreneur and making more money than I ever could at baseball.

But, that was a wonderful dream.

In real life, I was stuck. I had to have a party now. I'd really look like an idiot if I didn't. Besides, I could show off Teresa to my friends. I just didn't know when the house would be vacant. I

wouldn't have to break in through the basement. I had a key to get in. My mother didn't know it, but I found a set on the ground while visiting one time. George probably lost them.

George and John told me innocently about a horse show they were going to in Kentucky. That was just a week away, in late September. Perfect. It was also the same weekend as Mike Shannon's party on the next block.

I called Teresa about the party. With cell phones and Facebook these days, everyone learns about parties in a matter of a few hours. I had to use a payphone, which is something now almost extinct. Word of mouth had to do the rest. Teresa had no problem telling all her friends. My friends did the same thing. Actually, I wasn't worried about drawing a crowd. A little booze and food brings them out like flies.

The party was on. I figured a lot of people would go to Mike's party in the next block, but enough would come to mine. I spent most of the day buying snacks. I also ordered some subs and pizza for later on. Chris, who was over 21, picked up the beer kegs for us. David offered his stereo. I actually think he was proud I graduated. Besides, as Chris and Mike warned me, if I didn't invite David, he'd tell Mom what was going on.

Mom, George and John left the house around 10 a.m. Still, I waited to get things ready in the house until around 4 o'clock that afternoon, thinking that since Aunt Lisa lived on the next block, she might drive by to check on the house. At 6 p.m., the party started. Lots of kids from my old elementary school came along with my friends from high school. David seemed to be behaving.

I kept telling him to look out for anybody driving by to check on the house. As the night went on, a lot of people were coming over

from Mike's party by hopping the fence in the backyard. After a while, I found myself taking the same shortcut between the two parties.

Later on, I saw that Mike's party was winding down. I invited him and his remaining guests to join mine. By the time I returned, there must have been 300 people in the house.

Some of the girls were really friendly. Mary Sequin, who I thought was really hot, turned out to have a crush on Eric. However, Teresa couldn't keep her hands off me. She kept kissing me, too. Karen was friendly, too. The party would have been great even if just those two had shown up.

Mary Sequin and Renée Holland were getting way too drunk. They lived about 4 miles away. I figured I'd have to walk them both home.

Around midnight, I saw a car go by, it was my Aunt Lisa. I was really concerned, but she didn't stop. However, she could see the drapes were drawn, but the lights were on. I ended the party quickly and told everyone to go home before she came back around the block.

Everyone was gone, but Mary, Theresa and David when my aunt drove into the driveway. I told David to keep Renée downstairs behind the couch. I tried to hide Mary in the closet, but she was too drunk. I put her under the bed.

That was dumb. I realized I was in trouble. David and I weren't supposed to be there. Aunt Lisa knew that. I hoped we could come up with some plausible excuse.

"What are you kids doing in here?" Aunt Lisa, barked in a really pissed-off voice. That's when I realized it wasn't my Aunt Lisa, who would have been more understanding, but my Aunt Marion, who was older and less tolerant. I'd never seen her so mad. It didn't help that

Mary then puked all over the floor. I felt pretty bad, too. Uncle Charley and Aunt Marion had been the only members of the family to treat me like a person, and I had let them down.

I didn't argue as she yelled. She made David and me clean up Mary's vomit. Then, Aunt Marion told me that my mother was in the hospital. She hadn't gone to the horse show at all. I had no idea. She turned out to be all right.

After sprucing up the house, David and I walked the girls home. Chris came along because we'd been drinking, too. Back then the drinking age was 18. I wasn't going to drive. At least I had some good sense that night. Mostly, I was upset that I had lost my aunt and uncle's respect. I realized Charley wouldn't ask me to help him with any moving again. His son, Jerry, was now 13 and would take my job. In fact, Uncle Charley never called me again. Nor was I ever again invited to their house for dinner.

After that night was over, I couldn't wait to go back to work on Monday. We were going to start learning about different kinds of diseases trees can get and how to cure them with different pesticides.

The pain in my foot was nothing compared to the pain now in my heart. Sadly, I was responsible for both.

CHAPTER 13

I could only shrug off the past and focus on the future. I really felt I was on my way to a better destination. During the next several weeks, I continued to work for Davey Tree. With only a few weeks left to go in the apprenticeship, I decided to buy some warm clothes for the next winter. I actually had saved some money. Ken and Rose didn't charge me much rent, and I was making enough to feel confident. With my next paycheck, I planned to get some climbing gear I'd need for my job. Everything seemed like it was heading in the right direction. Of course, that didn't last long.

I went to a store off Ford Road where there happened to be a lot of construction at the intersection with Inkster Road. I bought winter overalls, gloves and work boots along with several pair of winter socks.

After walking to the corner, I saw a woman directing traffic through the construction, she motioned for me to go ahead and cross the street. Suddenly, I saw a tire rolling inches from my head and felt something hit me hard. A speeding truck had run the red light. I was thrown maybe 50 feet through the air. My tennis shoes were knocked

off my feet by the impact. I landed in a bloody heap and could not move my arms or legs. The woman directing traffic ran to my side. I couldn't talk to her or even acknowledge when she said the ambulance was coming.

I was taken to Oakwood Hospital, a familiar place. I woke up in a hospital bed completely puzzled by what had happened. My memory failed me. I think it's the mind's way of eliminating painful events. I recalled the tire and nothing else. Other people filled in details later. It's a wonder I survived. I definitely must've had a guardian angel looking after me. I had a cast on my right arm. My legs were in braces, my ribs hurt fiercely, and I had a terrible headache.

I was hooked up to monitors checking my heart, blood pressure and breathing. When a nurse came in, I finally learned that I had been run over by a drunk driver.

Dr. Gill stopped by that evening. He turned out to have been a student of Dr. Kim, who had taken care of my staph infection. He remembered my name. The doctor told me that I sustained a compound fracture of my arm along with badly bruised ribs, a severe concussion and compression fractures of the knees. I would have to stay in the hospital for a few days and would need physical therapy when I left. The only place I would be going for awhile was to Ken and Rose's house.

Over the next couple of days, insurance agents flocked to see me. I was rather innocent about insurance. I had some through Davey Tree, but really didn't understand the process. All I knew was that I would lose my job because I couldn't complete the training. The company wasn't going to let me re-enroll.

I didn't find much relief at home. Ken and Rose were constantly fighting. I knew it wasn't going to be long before they were going to ask

me to leave. I needed three months before the cast came off. Then, I hoped to find another job and a place to live in the winter. I didn't want to return to my car. That wasn't the destination I had in mind.

With time on my hands, movies developed into a great interest of mine. After all, make believe is a great way to escape for a while. Movies are made up of dreams. Through movies, you learn, you comprehend, you feel, and you expand your mind.

I have many favorites, including James Bond with Sean Connery, Pierce Brosnan and Daniel Craig saving the world and protecting her Majesty as a British secret agent double 007 with a license to kill, all with suave sophistication and rugged masculinity. And the famous introduction: "Bond… James Bond."

Then there's Gone With the Wind: a love story set in the South during the Civil War with Clark Gable as Rhett Butler and Vivian Leigh as Scarlett O'Hara who was romantically drawn to him. Both are pragmatists. The love-hate relationship proves that timing is everything

I also love Shakespeare's Romeo and Juliet. They are probably the most famous lovers ever, although their love story is tragic. Two teenagers fall in love at first sight and marry, bringing together two feuding families. The couple risks everything for their love. Taking your own life for your spouse is definitely a sign of true love.

I soon realized I didn't have to wish I was on a screen acting like them or dream about one day becoming an actor. I could create that world around me and live it. Movies opened my mind to another world, allowed me to pursue my passions. I learned how to love and be loved. Adventurer, world traveler, a crusader: my dreams became reality, leading me to appreciate life and to cherish the finer things in life, never to take anything or anyone for granted

There is only one happiness in life: to love and be loved. Love, like a river, will cut a new path. Whenever it meets an obstacle, love will always find a way into your heart. To the world you may be one person, but to one person. you may be the world. Love is the key that unlocks the bars of impossibility Love reminds you that nothing else really matters. You know you're in love when you see the world in her eyes and her eyes every-where in the world.

And my favorite: Love is strong yet delicate. It can be broken. To truly love is to understand this. To be in love is to respect this.

Kim, the agent for the insurance company of the truck driver, called and told me I was eligible to receive compensation for my lost wages from work for as long as I couldn't work or until the doctors said that I could go back to work. I knew nothing about suing the driver or the company and was simply pleased I'd be getting some compensation. I missed out on getting a lot of money by not filing a lawsuit. Later, when I learned that, I was surprised that a lawyer hadn't contact me. Someone else missed out on a big payday, too.

I made it through the winter even with Ken and Rose caterwauling on a regular basis. Friends talked about going to Florida for spring break. I wasn't so sure. I wanted to find another job or go to college to study architectural design and civil engineering. One friend, Gary, who had gotten me the job at the landscaping company, was persistent. Using the same non-stop technique I used on my mom, he wore me down. I finally agreed. At least it would be warm there. Besides, my arm still

wasn't strong enough to enable me to work. That meant I would continue to get monthly checks from the insurance company. On top of that, the trip did have some appeal. I quickly became excited about driving the 1,200 miles or so to Florida, the first of many trips to come. We dreamed of parties and eying the girls with their string bikinis walking along on the beach. We were going to paradise with white, sandy beaches that we could drive on, piers everywhere for fishing, cool crystal-blue waters, bright blue skies, parties raging all night and into the morning, and girls everywhere.

Who could resist that picture? Then, too, I knew someone in Florida: my grandmother had moved there with Chet. To be honest, I didn't want to see her, but she was family.

We left in mid-April for Daytona Beach, then a Mecca of spring break. Ft. Lauderdale was "where the boys are," according to the song, but we weren't looking for boys. We expected to stay about two weeks.

The image lived up to reality. Daytona Beach was great. We never even had to pay for a place to stay. Instead, two girls, Shelley and Selena, invited us to share their room in the Best Western hotel.

One night, Gary went out. Selena came back and fell asleep. So did I. The next morning, we found Shelley in her bed, but no Gary. Shelley said Gary had stayed at the pier at a party last night. I figured he would be back sometime. In the interim, Selena and I layed out at the beach and ended up looking like a couple of lobsters after a few hours. That night, Gary still did not return.

I combed the beach looking for Gary while Selena nursed her sunburn. I knew he could take care of himself, but I was his ride home. After four days, I called his dad, John, at the Garden Center back in Taylor to ask him if Gary had contacted him. He hadn't.

Finally, two days later, I got a call from a policeman. He told me Gary had been busted for selling pot and cocaine on the beach to an undercover cop. I denied knowing anything about that – which was completely true.

I never did any drugs other than a brief foray into marijuana. I despise people who become addicted to drugs and/or alcohol to escape reality. No matter how hard things were for me, no matter what obstacles I faced, no matter how much pain and suffering I endured, I knew I would never have been able to achieve success in life if I turned to drugs or alcohol. Life was hard enough, let alone trying to kick an addiction at the same time.

Gary needed $1,500 to post bond. I didn't have that kind of money, so I called his father again. John was angry, but said he'd catch the next plane to Daytona Beach. I said goodbye to Selena the next morning after having breakfast and walking along the beach with her. She was heading back to her home in West Virginia. Selena wrote me for a long time. I always wrote back. She loved me, and I cared for her very much. We would eventually meet again.

After she left, I drove home, grateful I had stayed in and not joined Gary that night. I would have been arrested, too. I never would see Gary again after our trip to Florida. I did hear that he would start hanging around the wrong people and would eventually end up in prison somewhere in Texas. Drugs probably led to his demise.

I was driving along through Cincinnati just across the Kentucky border on I-75 when my car started running rough. I thought I might have been running out of gas, but realized I still had half a tank. As steam began pouring from my engine about 300 miles from home, I started saying prayers that my car would make it. I finally crawled to

Ken and Rose's house. The car had a blown head gasket. That was going to cost about $800 to fix that. I didn't have that much money either.

I couldn't stay in the house since Ken and Rose were getting a divorce. Ken found me a place to stay with Helen Hallett, an elderly woman who was a friend of my father's side of the family. She needed help around her house. I could live with her and do housework, sort of like what David was doing with Pat and Henry without the sex. I ended up being the son Helen never had and stayed with her for two years. I thought of her as the mother I never had. She was about 80 and used an oxygen tank. I would drive her to the stores, and we would go shopping together.

If she needed anything during the week, she would ask me to pick it up. I did her chores, cut the lawn, trimmed the bushes and anything she needed in exchange for rent.

Ken came over weekly to check on us. He also was trying to sell his beautiful blue Dodge Charger so he could buy a truck. He wanted $3,000 for it, which I couldn't afford. However, he would let me pay for it at $100 a month. That was still too much because I knew the insurance checks were going to end. My physical therapist had told the insurance company that my arm was strong enough for me to work again.

However, my car was dying. I could barely drive it anywhere. I had no choice. I bought Ken's car and got a job working for Abundant Life Landscaping, which was owned by Dennis Ostopovich and his wife, Jeannie. I really enjoyed being there. Developing my all-around skills, I learned how to install brick, all kinds of retaining walls, boulders and stones, and how to build decks. I also learned all the materials that were available and how to design and install plants

in the field, not just on paper. Eventually, after a couple of years, I could look at a new house and draw a landscape design for customers just like a landscape architect..

Dennis and Jeannie were both devout Christians and ran their company on those principles. Ironically, Dennis was a big, strong guy who looked like a football player. Everyone was scared of him. On the other hand, Jeannie was the sweetest thing in the world. It wouldn't take long for us to become good friends.

Their survival story was inspirational. They both had recovered from very serious drug addictions. Dennis' teeth had been rotted by the drugs. Their complexions, like mine, were horrible, but they had been saved by the Lord Jesus Christ in their church, Brightmoor Tabernacle. They never touched drugs again. They had eight children, all with biblical names, and wanted more.

Their company now had more than 80 people on the payroll. In time, I started overseeing four of the company's eight crews for Dennis. As the boss, I enjoyed telling employees what to do and showing them how to do it. I taught them how to plant trees, lay sod, and install brick pavements and retaining walls. I was good at it and loved being in control. I would end up being the only one Dennis could find that was able to multitask and run multiple crews. Dennis and his wife said I was gifted.

Eventually, I began going to church on Sundays with them and attending Bible study. Dennis wanted to become a preacher one day and sometimes gave sermons at the Bible study. They even gave me the King James Version of the Bible, which I still carry with me today. The people at the church didn't seem like hypocrites like those I had met as a child at the Catholic Church. Dennis and Jeannie would invite me over their house after services. When we all sat

down to dinner, their kids would all say grace. The kids were all well mannered. Dennis and Jeannie lead by example and practiced what they preached.

I admired them for what they went through and respected them even more by the way they treated others. Their inner beauty shone through their actions and their big hearts. They were always there to help me and other people. They were real Christians.

I stayed for the next two years learning while I was living with Helen. My next door neighbor Mark Lapshan and I started going to clubs. He loved muscle cars like Monte Carlo SS and the Trans Am. Mark raced around the city in his Trans Am, but avoided tickets because his father used to be chief of police.

Like me, Mark wanted to make money. We'd watch the Three Stooges late at night and talk about how people were earning tons by working on Texas oil rigs. Mark said friends of his, Kevin and Julie, lived in Abilene about three hours south of Dallas. He was thinking of moving there. I knew working on an oil rig paid well although it was very dangerous work.

Finally, after many discussions, Mark grew tired of living at home and asked me if I want to go with him to Texas. I thought about it for a long time. I had some money saved, but knew I'd never get rich landscaping people's houses. I could feel the tug toward the rigs. I paid off Ken for the car and had to tell Dennis and Jeannie goodbye. They practically begged me to stay. It was very emotional. Dennis finally said I could always come back if things didn't work out. He understood: I was on a quest for riches, one that required me to move on.

It was especially hard for me to leave Helen, but I felt it was my future to make a lot of money as a roughneck. I told her I would

eventually come back and visit, and that I loved her and would miss her very much. She said she loved me and to call her once in awhile.

Neither Mark nor I knew what we were getting ourselves into. However, the compass of our lives pointed south. Daytona Beach had given me a taste of warm weather. I was ready to try someplace new. Two weeks later, we left for Texas. I left dreams of playing baseball behind. I left everything in my past behind. I had just turned 21 and finally, was going somewhere.

CHAPTER 14

We drove to Abilene and met Kevin and Julie. They turned out to be nice, but not much help getting us jobs on oil rigs. We didn't know where to start either and had no money. So, we both started working as bouncers at an Abilene bar and eventually moved over to Gillies, which is a famous bar.

While handling drunks and the occasional unruly customers, we would ask about working on oil rigs. A couple customers said drillers usually came in on Wednesday nights. Naturally, we were working Thursday through Sunday, the busiest days. We poked around until we got names of the drillers – Mitch and Cal, who were in charge of general operations for Red Ryder Drilling.

Meanwhile, Mark and I were enjoying celebrity status with the women in the bar. They liked bouncers. Mark went overboard and would bring a girl home every night. That got old listening to them while I was trying to sleep. I met a nice girl who was stationed at a nearby Air Force base. I dated her for a little while before she headed off on a tour of duty. She was easy to replace. There were plenty of nice girls. The girls back in Michigan had seemed stuck up. In Texas,

they were pretty and down to earth. I could have been biased: back home, I never had much time to date, but in Texas I was free for several days in a row. I loved every minute of it.

When Wednesday night rolled around, Cindy, the coat check girl, pointed out Mitch and Cal to us. They said they weren't hiring, but knew of a couple of drillers, Dale and John. Those were their real, names, but most people knew them as Seaweed and Cowboy. I was soon to find out that their nicknames fit them perfectly. They had just lost two deckhands or "worms" as they called them.

I was ready to jump at this opportunity, not knowing really how hard the work was going to be. The pay was the big incentive: $65 an hour, plus $45 a day for expenses' with $1 million free insurance.

Mark's eyes lit up and so did mine at that. All we saw were dollar signs. We both quit our jobs at the bar that night to start working for Red Ryder.

Neither one of us knew what we're getting ourselves into one of the most dangerous jobs in the country, at any given time, we could be killed.

This job was not my career choice. By now, I had decided I would rather be a lawyer. Unfortunately, I couldn't afford to go to college and didn't have the time anyway. However, I realized I could make more money working in the oil industry. That's how an entre-preneur thinks. I was becoming one.

The rigs functioned 24 hours a day. There were different kinds of rigs based on size: single, double, triple or quad. The larger the rig the deeper we could drill by using more than one piece of pipe at a time. Rigs were used based on the depth of the drilling and terrain. Each rig contained a diverse crew.

- The derrick hand was responsible for the "mud," the water or oil-based mud pits where drilling fluids circulated around the system, and the mud pump. He monitored the mud weight (density), added sacks of chemicals to the mud to maintain properties, and monitored the mud level in the mud pits to aid in the well control. He was housed in the derrick about 110 feet off the ground while tripping pipe and would rack drill pipes by mast alongside the derrick.

- The driller was responsible for his crew. He made sure everything was running smoothly and controlled the rig's machinery during drilling and most other rig operations.

- The tool pusher was in charge of overseeing all operations on a land-drilling rig. On off-shore oil rigs, he was in charge of the drilling department. He reported to the master or OIM (depending on the company) who then reported to the shore-based rig manager. Other department heads include the Chief Mate and Chief Engineer etc. The tool pusher maintained all the necessary tools and equipment and supplies, and worked in conjunction with the company man. If anything broke he would fix it. Naturally, his nickname was Bulldog.

- A company man represented the oil drilling company. Oil drilling companies typically rent or lease rigs from another company that owned the rig and hired the majority of the personnel on the drilling rig. The company man was directly in charge of most operations pertain-

ing to the actual drilling and integrity of the wellbore. While the well is being drilled, the company man must rely on the well site geologist (or mud logger) to inform him if the well is dry or if it's going to be a producer. The real expert from an investor's standpoint is the mud logger.

- The mud logger is typically contracted by the oil company or operator. His or her tasks are primarily to gather data by collecting samples during drilling to identify possible indications of hydrocarbons. Mud loggers observed and interpreted indicators in the mud returns during the drilling process. At regular intervals, the mud logger logged properties such as drilling rate, mud weight, flowline temperature, natural gas content and type, oil indicators, pumps pressure, pump rate, and the rock type of the drill cuttings. Sampling the drill cuttings was performed at predetermined intervals and was difficult during rapid drilling.

- When the derrick hand wasn't tripping pipe or if I was not busy, we would sometimes go below the rig and take samples for the mud logger to analyze the next day.

The logging sometimes started the day drilling began, known as the "spud in" date. It was more likely they would start as the drilling reached a certain depth. Mud loggers would connect various sensors to the drilling apparatus and install specialized equipment to monitor or log drill activity. This required precise calibration and alignment to provide accurate readings.

However, I thought one of the most important tasks of the mud logger was to monitor gas levels and notify other personnel if gas levels may be reaching dangerous levels so appropriate steps can be taken to avoid a dangerous well blow out. This kept everyone as safe as could be expected.

- Each rig also had three roughnecks. Their duties included anything involved with the connecting and sliding pipe down the well hole. They were also responsible for the general labor around the rig. Despite such responsibilities, they were the lowest paid. That was Mark and me.

We would have to drive a couple hours each day to get out to the oilfields just outside of Abilene. That wasn't a problem for Mark with his Trans Am. He would cruise along at about 120 mph each way.

There was nothing to stand in our way, just a wide-open road and roaming tumbleweeds in cotton fields. It was like Smokey and the Bandit, only with no Smokies around.

The company was getting ready to move the rig to another location when we showed up on our first day. A couple miles down the road, we set up a double rig. That meant we could drill two pipes at a time and trip two pipes at a time for a total of about 60 feet each time. After we hit 60 feet, we would add another 60 feet until hitting gas or oil.

Before the rig was installed, three different holes often had to be drilled: the conductor, rathole, and mouse hole. The conductor hole was a large-diameter hole, lined with pipe and drilled by a portable

drilling rig. Also called a starter hole, it varied in depth down to tens of feet to a few hundred feet depending on the geology. Some sites do not require a conductor hole.

The rat-hole was in the rig floor, 30 to 35 feet deep, lined with casing that projected above the floor. The pipe was placed inside it when hoisting operations were in progress. The mouse hole was under the rig floor, usually lined with pipe, in which joints of drill pipe were temporarily placed. These two holes could be drilled by the primary rig.

Mark and I worked on a rig that used Hydraulic Rotary drilling, which utilized a three-cone roller, fixed cutter diamond, or diamond-impregnated drill bits to wear away at the cutting surface. Using these methods for drilling is preferred because the objective is to strike a deep formation containing oil or natural gas. The machinery enabled the pipe to penetrate several miles deep with rotating, hollow drill pipes carrying bentonite and barite to lubricate, cool, and clean the drilling bit. The mud then traveled to the surface around the outside of the drilling rods. Another form of well logging was electronic, which resembled a seismograph.

These techniques could both be done while the well was being drilled. When the well hole was finished, we could lower measurement tools into the newly drilled hole.

After a conductor hole, rat-hole, and mouse hole were complete, we began setting up the rig. Mark and I carried most of the work load until we proved ourselves and gained the experience we needed. To keep any contamination away from the freshwater, we dug a trench all the way around the rig, which was horrible and very difficult work. We used picks. We couldn't use shovels because the ground was so hard. We then helped place a blow-out preventer on top of the

conductor hole or rathole. It weighed tons and had to be perfectly aligned with and through the drilling deck. Once that was done, we attached the drill bit on to the pipe and dropped our first pipe down in through the hydraulic deck.

Roughly about every 20 minutes to a half hour, we would add more pipe. Initially, most of the time, we wouldn't use a blow-out preventer. However, it became standard practice because there were too many accidents happening on oil rigs all over the state of Texas. Unfortunately, it wasn't much help if you were drilling for oil and hit a gas pocket. If that happened, gas pressure in the pocket would explode, creating a crater-like hole that sucked in the oil rig and killed everybody on the rig and anyone nearby. This was the most dangerous part of the job. It seemed like every other week, we were hearing about a rig that blew out and killed everyone. Sometimes, if they were lucky, some survived, but, most of the time, no one did.

There were other ways to get hurt from all the steel. You can't hurt or kill steel, but it can hurt and even kill you. All we could do was throw it, control it, overpower it and get mad at it. Nothing weighed less than 200 pounds. We also had to "throw chain." Today, government regulations have made this illegal because it's so dangerous, but this was 40 years ago.

After tripping miles of pipe out of the ground, I would be standing on the driller's side of the floor. I had to wrap a chain around the bottom pipe, attach the new piece of pipe and "throw" the chain to make it jump to the new piece before drawing in the chain to fully attach the new piece of pipe.

The chain often whipped around, knocking out teeth, gashing heads or killing worms. I also had to hope that I didn't get my hand caught in between the pipe and the chain. Inserting the sleeve and

snapping the heavy tong-like forks that wrapped around the pipe happened within a matter of seconds. If I were not precise, my partner and I were going to get hurt or killed.

After we were done drilling a hole and reached oil or gas, the casing crew would show up. The casing pipe was larger in diameter and longer than drill pipe and is used to line the hole. Casing operations occur periodically throughout the drilling process. After the casing is in place, drilling fluid is circulated through it to remove any residual gases and to condition the mud. After circulating and conditioning the mud, the casing is cemented. During this process, the casing is rotated to allow the workers to remove excess wall cake to give the cement a better bond. Once this had been accomplished, the company would decide to make whether or not to cap the well or to make it a producer. Capping off the well was easy; you would just put a ventilated seal on the casing. Otherwise, the oilfield pump techs would hook up the pump and start production

Often, another shift helped out with casing. Occasionally, a couple guys from our crew would stay over and help them lift the casing on to the rig floor with a crane.

Once our job was finished, we would move to the next site to start drilling and then repeat the process all over again.

Mark only lasted a year before he quit and moved into installing prefab homes. He just couldn't take the long hours, the strenuous, constant heavy lifting and the risks. The fear of a blow out was too much. Mark told me I was crazy and had a death wish because I would continue working on the oil rig. I didn't feel that way.

I was willing to endure the long hours and the fears that came along with the job. I had learned to cope with anything.

I never had time to be afraid or worry about what could happen. My mind was always focused on getting the job done and just getting through the day. I always used to say to myself the usual mantra: another day, another dollar.

Nobody cared what happened to me anyway. There was nobody to come home to, nobody to talk to. Helen called to tell me she missed me, but no one else.

This was my life now, and I was making a lot of money. But, I didn't like who I was becoming. The job was so demanding. It required so much strength and determination just to get through the day. I was working in pain every day because of my muscles were so overworked and fatigued. My muscles were not repairing themselves fast enough. The job was also making me mean. Nevertheless, I wouldn't stop. I knew greater pain when I was younger under my mother's rule. I was always working in pain at any job I had before. I was determined that nothing could stand in my way. There was never a job too hard for me or one I thought I couldn't handle.

Working hard kept my mind focused and my dreams alive. Most of all, I couldn't get into trouble. I didn't have time to do anything, but work.

I worked so long so hard that, sometimes, I wouldn't even have time to come home and take a shower or even take my overalls off. I was so exhausted. I would just sit in the wooden rocking chair on the front porch and just fall asleep, then the next morning, wake up and do it all over again.

I continued working in the oil fields over the next few years until around the mid-1980s when the bottom started falling out of the oil industry in Texas and around the world. The United States started to fall into recession. Soon, oil companies went out of business

throughout the state of Texas. Others survived by laying off workers. I was one of them.

Now 24 years old with some money in the bank, I went back to Michigan and moved in with Helen. Mark stayed behind. I hated to leave since he was my only friend, but I wasn't interested in working in construction at that time. The money was nowhere close to the pay I was making on the oil rigs.

Back in Michigan, I tried to find a job working on the oil rigs there. I quickly realized most jobs were up north around Cadillac and Kalkaska, at least 3 1/2 hours by car from my house in Allen Park. If I could find a job on an oil rig working for a company, it would have been worth the drive. I would just stay up there during the week and come home on the weekends to help Helen around the house, do her grocery shopping or whenever she needed.

After traveling up north several times, I finally found TD Province Drilling located out of Mt. Pleasant. The company was drilling throughout with triple rigs, which meant it was drilling deep.

I filled out an application, but the company didn't plan to fill any positions for a few weeks. That gave me time to recover. I had no idea it would also give me the chance to head in a totally different direction on a personal level.

CHAPTER 15

While I was enjoying the time off from the rig, I figured I would get in touch with some of my childhood friends. I was only able to reach Chris. We went out to a Taylor bar called Drinks Saloon. Despite the name, I didn't drink anything but couple of Cokes that night; neither did Chris. We went up there to play pool, talk about old times and, of course, to check out the ladies while listening to the DJ playing music. Chris was working full time at a gypsum plant making drywall. He said that Mike and Eric had full-time jobs working for a moving company and that they were doing quite well.

We spent our time looking backwards, when, as it turns out, I should have been looking ahead.

I started feeling like I was being watched. There definitely were a lot of girls. I noticed one in particular who was staring at me. I stared back. Tall and thin, she just smiled and sipped on her beer. She continued smiling at me every time I looked at her. I thought she was so beautiful and her smile so bright. Her face glowed as she smiled. With her brown eyes lit up, and long, wavy black hair, she looked like a sexy, sultry Latin girl with a body just to die for. Of course, Chris thought she would go for him, but she told him she liked me. I don't know why, but I couldn't take my eyes off her. And, she kept staring at me.

I didn't know what to do. I never dated anyone. I thought that money was everything the most important thing. Girls didn't make me money; they made me spend money. I was so focused on making money. I still had my mind set on becoming a millionaire by age 30. I believed the world was based on money. If you didn't have money, you had nothing; you were a nobody. I wasn't about to be a nobody.

I didn't think anybody could ever love me unless I had money. With money came respect and power. I really didn't know what love was since I never had been loved. What was love?

Yet, I felt something about this woman. Finally, my curiosity overcame my shyness. I went over to her and introduce myself. I walked up to her and said in a different voice, "My name is Bond, James Bond." She couldn't stop laughing. Right then, I knew she really liked me.

After she was done laughing and almost choking on her beer, she said her name was Katrina. She was 24, the same age as me.

Chris went home early while Katrina and I stayed until closing, getting to know one another. She said she worked as an account manager for the accounting department for a company named Textron Acceptance Corp. in Farmington Hills. I told Katrina that I worked on the oil rigs as a roughneck. She lived in Plymouth, which was about a 20-minute drive on the freeway from where I was living with Helen in Allen Park.

The time flew by. As we were talking, I could see that she was an incredible woman, exuberant, full of energy and fun to be around. The bar was getting ready to close. Since we were both hungry, we went to a restaurant called the Silver Dollar across the street. We ended up there for breakfast and talking some more. Then, she asked me if I wanted to go home with her. She said that her parents were over in Europe. Nobody was home. They traveled a lot, she said. By that time, I knew things would never be the same.

Katrina was paying attention to me, laughing and giggling with me, having fun. She liked the same things that I liked to do. I'd never

met anyone who treated me like this. I almost didn't know how to act around her.

I ended up going home with her that night. The next morning, we both knew what we felt for each other. It was the compassion and kindness that she showed me. No one had ever showed me that before.

Was this love? I thought it was. That weekend, we spent talking about our goals and dreams, and what we wanted to achieve out of life. Katrina told me that she had been adopted. She had two other brothers who were also adopted Dennis and Charles. Katrina had everything, especially good parents who adopted her. She had traveled everywhere in Europe with her parents. They treated her like she was their own biological daughter.

I noticed a lot of pictures hung on walls around her house. One picture showed a couple who looked like her grandparents. It turned out to be her parents. They seemed much older than other parents for our age. She said that they were in their mid-60s. Her father, Lloyd Gilder, worked for Ford Motor Co. as an executive for advertising and traveled a lot over in Europe. That is where he met her mother, Ivana. She was from Hungary, a very poor country.

Being an American citizen, Lloyd was able to marry Ivana and bring her back to the United States to live. Katrina said that her mother never could have children. Ivana eventually became a United States citizen herself.

Katrina told me that her parents were very controlling over her. I told her I could see why. I told her that if she were my daughter and as beautiful, I would do the same. I soon found out that her mother would take protection to extremes.

I told her that I have been on my own since 13 and that my aspirations were that, one day, I would be rich, famous and powerful, and able to help the poor kids achieve their dreams and goals. I couldn't do that without owning my own business. I said to Katrina that God would show me the way. I just had to listen.

Her parents weren't due home for another week. I spent the whole week with Katrina in her house. I could hardly wait to meet

her parents. I thought what loving compassionate parents they must be to adopt three children and raise them as their own. I could see why Katrina was so compassionate, so loving, so caring, but I also learned she was very naïve. Katrina said her mom and dad sheltered her and protected her all her life from the real world more than her brothers. When I finally met her parents, I realized why they were so protective of Katrina, especial her mother. She had survived World War II concentration camps during the Holocaust as well as famine. As a result, Katrina's mother had witnessed some horrible things in Europe throughout Hungary. It's not a wonder that she wanted to shield her daughter.

We dated for a couple months now and tried to find a way to live together. We were so much in love with each other. Katrina not only inspired me, but I knew she would work alongside me to achieve the same things out of life that we wanted.

One day, her parents asked Katrina to invite me for dinner. They had to be wondering who this man was that their daughter just couldn't stop talking about. I was glad for the chance to be with her. Since her parents returned from Europe, Katrina had to be home at a set time. Her mother also had her constantly doing something. We couldn't see each other as much as we wanted. I was always thinking of ways to be with her, to love her, to hold her. I was anxious and nervous to meet her parents. I didn't know what they would think of me.

I could only be myself. I was very nervous. As I sat down around the table, Lloyd seemed very quiet and down to earth. Tall with a slender build and the salt-and-pepper hair of an older gentleman, he appeared very distinguished and didn't talk much. Ivana, on the other hand was a pistol, full of energy. She asked me all sorts of questions in a Hungarian accent. What kind of the job did I have? Where did I live? How did I plan on taking care of her daughter? She just wouldn't stop talking. I didn't have to guess who wore the pants in that family as Lloyd just sat there listening. Some of the questions were just preordained as though she was trying to run me off. That just wasn't going to happen. After

dinner, we sat around watching TV while I answered additional questions.

I told both Katrina's parents that I had great dreams and was full of aspirations. I was waiting to hear from an oil company in Cadillac to start work on a rig and that, eventually, I wanted to own my own business. I knew that this was the only way I would have total control over my destiny. I told them about my working experience, Helen and my life to date.

After a few weeks, I noticed it was getting harder and harder to be with Katrina. I couldn't figure out why at first, but then she told me. Her parents didn't think that I was good enough for her and were try to keep her away from me. That made me mad. No one was going to keep me from being with Katrina as long as she felt the same way towards me. Now, more than ever, I wanted to prove to her parents that I was worthy of her.

To succeed, I needed to open up my own landscape company. I would do landscaping during the day and move furniture at night. I was very good at those two professions. Since landscape construction was only seasonal, I could move furniture in the winter. I told her I would work 24 hours a day, seven days a week if necessary to fulfill my goal of being a millionaire by the time I was 30.

Nevertheless, after couple more months, Katrina was not able to see me anymore. At this point, I gave Katrina an ultimatum: either join me or stay with her parents. I had talked to Helen to see if Katrina could move in with me. She was also very fond of Katrina and thought of her as her daughter. She agreed. I was sure Katrina would leave and come live with me since she wanted away from her parents' rules. And she did.

I wanted to be rich and powerful, help others that were in need and less fortunate. I would veer away from trouble. Someone would always be watching over me – a guardian angel throughout the time I should have been dead. I knew all the despair, hardships and disappointments, were preparing me for something larger than life, training, teaching learning to become humble modest and wise to

become a leader to teach and lead others by example. Always coming away with something positive, learning a lesson from a setback or a tragedy. In a negative, you will always find something positive. It is a state of mind.

So, the journey begins with someone that loves me, someone I looked forward to being with for the rest of my life. In return, I would love her.

I was ready to open my own business, but needed a name for it. Actually, I had no trouble coming up with one. I have always been intrigued by movies, TV soaps and stories. One of most famous, popular and long-running television drama series was called Dynasty, which ran between 1981 and 1989. Blake Carrington and Alexis Colby were the names of the main characters who headed rival companies. I was intrigued mainly because Dynasty was based on rich and famous oil businesses. I was into that because of my work on oil rigs.

The show was fascinating with its emphasis on the material things that they were able to buy with their money, and the power to wheel everything to their advantage. Scheming, plotting, engineering: the perfect plan to keep family members one step ahead of each other.

I loved the name Carrington, the power, the money and the scheming, but not the backstabbing and gossip. I prefer to say something directly to someone, not behind his or her back, or I would go to the source. That's what real professional men and women do. Nevertheless, Dynasty not only moved me, it motivated and inspired me. It drove me. I needed a powerful name behind my company to get people's attention. This is the way anyone with a business has to think. Carrington became the name of my company. Carrington echoed, power, money adventure, excitement and, most of all, class.

It also became my name. Changing my name had been a consideration for a long time. Before I had ever met anyone and fell in love, I knew I wouldn't want to be married to anyone or have kids with the last name Pickle. That's for sure. I didn't want little "dills" running

around. I definitely didn't want them to ever have problems going through school or growing up that I had. I had the perfect setting to alter my name. I would use it to my advantage.

I asked several attorneys on how I could change my name. They advised me to file the appropriate papers through probate court where a judge approved the change. I have now carried the last name Carrington with pride since I was 24 years old I was so proud after the judge approved the switch. I shed more than two decades off my life that day. I was putting everything behind me, letting everything go that hurt me in the past and held me back. My mother no longer had a grip on my emotions or my feelings. I let her go right along with my old name.

The name change had another positive effect: I took all my internal anger and turned it into constructive energy. No longer would I let the people who would say I couldn't do this, I couldn't do that affect me. I would get away from them. Those people can't do anything for themselves and never amounted to anything in their own lives. I would prove them wrong every time.

I went down to the County building and filed papers to start my company. Naturally, I called it Carrington Landscaping and Building Maintenance. I knew I couldn't run a business from Helen's house. She needed more quiet time. Moreover, Katrina told me she was pregnant. When she did, all of a sudden my heart seemed to stop. Being raised Catholic, I thought I was doing the right thing by marrying her before the baby was born. We found a home in Garden City, Michigan. We moved in and were married by the mayor there. I started the business and my family virtually simultaneously.

My next investment was in advertising in my new company. I knew that wealthy people who would want my services lived in Bloomfield Hills, Farmington, Franklin and throughout the rest of Oakland County, which is one of the biggest and richest counties in the country. I had three ways to reach them:

- Marriage mailing, which consists of combining my advertising with ads from many other companies and sending them out in one mailing.

- Circular advertising, which involves placing a flyer inside a newspaper.

- Direct mailing, which means mailing an ad directly to a selected home. This is the best way by far.

Unfortunately, I didn't have enough money for any of that. So, I designed a flyer describing my company's services. Then, I relied on the fourth advertising method. It's called finding the way to accomplish a goal without having any money. That described me perfectly.

I had 100,000 81/2 x 11 flyers printed. I then proceeded to buy a county-by-county map with all the zip codes streets and addresses. Each day, I would hop into my truck and put flyers inside mailboxes. Every day, 6,000 to 10,000 flyers were placed into mailboxes. I'm not recommending anyone do this, because it is against the law to put flyers in a mailbox. I could legally stick flyers in doors, but didn't have the time to go door-to-door. I was lucky; I got away with it. As long as I didn't get a phone call from the Post Office telling me to stop, I continued. Actually, I didn't get called until a few years later even though my phone number was on every flyer. I was told to stop or face prosecution. By then, it didn't matter.

After the first month of spring, potential customers started calling. I was soon averaging about 20 to 30 estimates a day. I started out with one crew of three and quickly grew to three crews. The fourth crew was with me. This was definitely not the time to be shy. With the last name of Carrington, people were always comparing me to the

prime-time soap opera. I guess 95 percent of the people I talked to asked me if I were related to the characters. It paid off to have a bold and powerful name.

That first month I grossed $20,000. Back then, that was a lot of money. That wasn't net, however, which was what was left after I paid expenses. I paid $3000 for gas and tools, and $2,000 for employees. That means I posted a $15,000 profit. That money was used to buy more equipment or vehicles as well as pay for household expenses. I usually split income in half between the business and the house. It's very important to put as much money as possible into expanding your business.

I funneled some of the cash into more advertising. For several years, I delivered the flyers directly. After I saved enough for direct mail, I bought a bulk mailing permit for a couple hundred dollars.

After the flyers were printed, the printer applied the bulk mailing stamp. I used mailing lists purchased from companies that collected names. That was a lot quicker than driving around and a lot easier on both the body and the vehicles.

My business thrived. I learned to interact with people, how to read their expressions. I communicated enthusiasm. They saw I was excited about doing the job and shared their passion. I described exactly, what steps I would take to accomplish their job and how long it would take from start to finish. I spoke to customers with conviction, leave them with no doubt that I could do a better job than anyone else. I looked at them directly in the eyes and was completely honest.

I meant every word. I wanted to create a good life for my wife, my kid and for myself. I would never look back, only forward. I knew there would be many obstacles in my path trying to achieve success. I

also realized this wouldn't be the only endeavor I would undertake. There would be many.

For each, I followed the same philosophy. I heard a lot of people say it takes money to make money. That is not really true. It takes determination, the will to overcome all odds. Where there's a will, as you've heard, there's a way. You will find that way, especially when failure is not an option.

Along with that steely approach, I had to think of every method possible to save money. One choice was to do a lot of the work myself so I didn't have to pay an employee. Any money I saved was money in my pocket.

For example, although I was making money during the six-to-seven month season, I also was losing too much by having to pay for repairs of vehicles and equipment. To save money, I started doing the repairs myself.

If I didn't know how to replace a part, I bought books to find out how. There are books to teach you how to do anything. I had already learned a lot by working on cars when I was younger. I could take anything apart and be able to put it back together from scratch. Having a photographic memory definitely came in handy. It also helped that I wasn't afraid to repair things on my own or learn how. I ended up saving thousands of dollars. As a result, my first season was a successful only because I learned to save money by doing work I could by myself.

In the fall, with winter approaching, my daughter, Britney, was born. That was the happiest day of my entire life. At that very moment as I watched Katrina deliver her, I realized how beautiful life really is and what life is all about. It is a gift from God: so beautiful, perfect, so precious, so innocent. The love surrounded me, engulfed

me and mesmerized me. I thought how beautiful my child is and how powerful God is. I will never forget that day, nor would anyone. A baby is so dependent on us as parents to protect them, nurture them, to guide them. My life changed forever in just those few moments as my daughter was brought into this world. Nicole followed two years later, in 1988, and my son, Blake, came in 1991. I decided all of them would have all the material that the characters on Dynasty had – and everything I lacked as a child.

CHAPTER 16

During my second year in business, I met someone that became very influential in my life as a mentor and father figure. His name was Ron Bleckman. He lived in Farmington Hills. I simply put a flyer in his mailbox. I would've never guessed how our relationship would end up after that.

One day, Ron and his wife, Cookie, called me, setting in motion the most prosperous relationship I've ever known. I would work with Ron and Cookie for more than 18 years before our relationship ended abruptly.

Throughout the first 15 years, I would work every summer and sometimes through the winter on their house, occasionally going to Florida to work on the home they own in West Palm Beach. There was plenty of room: the Farmington address was three acres with an extra lot next door. I did everything from landscaping and remodeling to installing a nine-hole golf course in their yard with built-in sprinkling systems to erecting a bridge across the Rouge River in their backyard.

It was a full-time job just taking care of the yard, decks and gaze-bos, from painting to removing over 100 huge ash trees that died from ash borer disease. You name it; I did it for them. They did not need to look any further for anyone else to do the work. I made sure they didn't have to. I never turned down any job they wanted done. Nothing was too hard or too easy, too large or too small. If I didn't know how to do something, I would spend a day learning how to do it. The next day, I was able to do the job and do it well. They liked that. All that from just one flyer, one of thousands distributed that day and every day. That little piece of paper changed my life

I needed the work. Running the business and raising three chil-dren definitely took a toll on our family budget. It was very difficult. I had to figure out other ways to make money. So, I entered other skill trades: construction, remodeling homes, building driveways, patios, decks, excavating, plumbing, electrical. Whatever was necessary, I would learn it.

I developed a sure-fire technique to get the proper experience. I would take an ad out in the local newspaper to hire someone for that specific job or task I needed to accomplish. I would pay him as a subcontractor, which means he was paid for that specific job and nothing more. Then I would watch and work with him. By the time that job was done, I knew how to do it myself. I was never afraid that I would make mistakes. I would just do it over until I got it right. You can't be afraid of screwing up something. This is how you will learn from your mistake, and you will become better at accomplishing your task. In time, the more jobs you do, the more time you do it, you will become an expert. I was able to watch some of the toughest jobs being done by other workmen and able to do them the next day with ease. I learned a lot of my skills through a lot of my clients

throughout the years working at Ron and Cookie's house. As Dennis and Jeannie Ostopovich once told me, I was really gifted. Now, I was learning to use my ability. Everyone is gifted in different ways. All you have to do is find out what you do best

While I was learning the skill trades, I would contract jobs, allowing me to make additional money at the same time. In the winter, I would have to fall back on moving furniture to make ends meet. As a result, I visited almost all 50 states and traveled from coast to coast. I would eventually get my chauffeur's license, so I could drive tractor-trailers. Today it's called a CDL or commercial driver's license.

All this work, watching and learning started to take a toll on our marriage. I didn't quite understand at the time what was going on. I still needed to make more money in a time when many families were beginning to require two incomes. Katrina was a housewife, raising the children, so I had to be the one earning money.

The years went by so fast. In the 1990s, everything seemed different: economy, household income, morality, and the dynamics of an American married couple. The cost of living was rising rapidly. I did not see how Katrina was being affected by the changing world. I was just glad she stayed home with the children. There are many benefits for us because she took care of the kids:

It was hard to find a babysitter that we could trust; and daycare was too expensive. Besides, I believe that only Mom could provide the necessary nurturing and bonding.

On the other hand, Katrina complained the kids were driving her crazy. However, they always behaved for me. I told her she wasn't disciplining them enough. She was letting them get away with everything with no consequences.

If that wasn't bad enough, I wasn't spending enough time with her. Although I loved her very much, I was too busy thinking of the future and building a business while providing for our kids. I thought she understood my thinking, but that wasn't good enough. I was obsessed with money and my own personal gain, to be independently wealthy. I knew if I could reach that goal, we could live a rewarding life and never have to worry about money again. My kids would be happy. I wanted to take care of them completely. Also, I never gave up hope that, one day, I could help abused children, encourage, inspire and motivate them and show them that someone loves them.

There were other concerns, too, other than paying the bills and taking care of my family. I was running into trouble with the law. I hired an attorney to protect me and my business. After being charged with larceny by conversion, a dispute over the material, I paid the supplier to settle the case. On other occasions, a couple clients sued me.

That was a very difficult time while I was raising children and trying to please my wife, too.

I knew we had problems in our marriage. I even heard whispers that she was having an affair. I didn't believe them. I thought that money would cure everything. It would get me away from all the difficulties. It would bring dreams and fantasies to reality. I wanted money and lots of it. I figured I would try to buy my way out of any problem. We usually rented a house, for example, but I thought owning one would bring Katrina and me closer together. I always wanted to dabble in real estate anyway. Now I would have my chance.

It would have to be a nice house. I would settle for nothing less. I was sure a large, imposing house would help Katrina respect me

more. I spent about three weeks looking in the newspaper for land contract. That way we would own the house and make the payments to the seller, rather than to a bank. I didn't have enough credit at the time to finance it through a financial institution anyway. I finally found a home in Troy with four bedrooms, 2 1/2 baths, an attached garage and a huge backyard to play. Earl, the owner, agreed to hold the mortgage. We moved in soon after.

Unfortunately, that only made things worse. Not only were the finances killing us, but we were living in a $350,000 house in Sylvan Glen, a very wealthy neighborhood. Most of the neighbors didn't feel that I had the right to even live in that subdivision. I was so young, and they were middle-aged.

On top of that, Katrina started acting strangely. She started leaving the house at odd hours and not coming home until early in the morning. I started wondering what was going on. So, one night, I hired one of the neighborhood kids to babysit while I went looking for her. I didn't know if this was a very good idea or not or what I would find out, but I do remember it was a cold night in the fall. I figured she would go downriver, which was about 40 miles away. That's where all her friends lived. I drove around for hours, looking for her Lincoln Town car. I went to bars, hotels, friends' homes and anywhere else I thought she might be.

Finally, I found the car in a hotel parking lot. I went into a manager's office to see if she was registered there. She was. I said I was her husband, and the manager gave me the room key. I was getting nervous, and my heart started beating faster. I had no idea what was going on.

I walked up to the room door. My wife certainly didn't know that the manager had given me the key. I unlocked the door and walked

into the room. I saw her purse, but she wasn't there. I figured she was probably at one of the bars across the street from the hotel. I decided to hide behind the shower curtain and wait for her to come back.

About three in the morning, I heard somebody at the door. At this point, my heart was racing. I wouldn't believe what I saw next. My brother David walked through the door with her. I was furious, ready to kill him.

I confronted them. "What the hell are doing in a hotel room with my brother?" I asked her angrily.

"Nothing," she kept saying.

I looked over at my brother. "What the hell are you doing here with my wife?" I asked him.

No answer he could give would appease me. I knew he was sleeping with her. I lost control and kicked the shit out of him. All the years of resentment exploded. I was like Henry years ago who discovered David with his wife, Pat. Only I didn't have a gun. I finally dangled him from the third floor over the railing, ready to drop him down onto the parking lot. At that moment, it flashed through my mind that if I killed him, I would go to prison, and my kids wouldn't have a father. I knew what growing up without a father was like. I brought him back over the railing and stomped out.

I realized then my wife couldn't be trusted at all. On top of that, a couple of my friends knew that David had been sleeping with Katrina and didn't tell me until after the hotel confrontation. I even caught them in the act on another occasion. She eventually stole a check from my business account, made it out to herself, cashed it and gave the money to David to go to Tucson, Arizona to stay with her mom and dad. I found the ticket receipts.

Stuck in the house by myself, I tried to sell it. I demanded a non-refundable deposit. One couple finally put down the required $3,500 deposit and filled out the land contract agreement.

In the midst of all the chaos, I was trying to do everything legally. However, I didn't know that Earl had to get permission from the bank to sell me the contract. It was an exclusive deal. I did not know this until he had found out that I had sold the house on land contract to some other folks. He came over and wanted me to sign a quick claim deed, releasing the house back to him. I told him I had already sold the home.

He was very upset. He said he owned and sold several homes this way. Each bank would demand payment if it found out what he had done. He asked me to save his ass. He said he would let me out of the $5,000 dollars that I owed him. In turn, he wouldn't ruin my credit. I thought it over and thought that my buyers may not have good credit. They could lose their deposit. I signed a quick claim to the house and returned ownership back to Earl. If necessary, I would just return the deposit to the potential buyers.

However, Katrina stole all the money that I had in the bank. Then, she left and took the kids to go out to Arizona, too. I didn't know what to do. I was broke. I had no house, no money to refund the potential buyers. And my wife and kids had left the state.

Finally, Uncle Charlie and Aunt Marion offered me a place to stay at their home. That's where I ended up going.

I missed the kids terribly. They were my life, my joy and my world. I refused to think that they would be brought up without a father as I had been. The thought of a failing marriage and divorce looming over me was equally awful. Failure wasn't in my vocabulary. I hadn't given up on before, and I wouldn't now.

I will never forget the day I told my aunt and uncle that I would leave for Arizona to pick up Katrina and the kids and head to Florida. Uncle Charlie told me to leave them there. Their grandparents will take care of them. He said that I should stay in Michigan, take care of my business and start a new life. I disagreed. I knew if Katrina continued with the divorce, she would take everything from me in alimony alone. I had to try to resolve this. If I leave, my uncle said, I couldn't come back. I should've listened.

I left everything to drive 5,000 miles. I picked up Katrina and our three children and drove to Clearwater, Florida. We stayed in a hotel while trying to find a house to live. I forgot all about the deposit I owed to the people who had wanted to buy the house in Troy.

We took the kids to Disney We visited all the theme parks. Katrina enjoyed it, too. All I could think about was trying to save our marriage for the kids' sake.

I was never worried about finding a job or money. I knew how to do everything. United Van Lines would end up contracting me to drive their tractor-trailer to move furniture across the state of Florida. This would allow me to see virtually every city in Florida.

We lived in Florida for almost a year before the unthinkable happened. On my way to work, a sheriff pulled over my car. I was told there was a warrant for the arrest of Katrina and me. We were going to jail. Our three kids were abruptly placed into a foster home. This was a life-altering moment that turned into an life-changing event.

The charge was that we hadn't returned the deposit on the Troy house. We would eventually be extradited from Florida to Michigan to answer on charges of fraud. Our kids were left behind somewhere in Florida. Our car impounded, and we were in jail. Eventually, we were released on personal bond until the court proceedings. I

promptly headed down to Florida to pick up the kids. How ashamed I felt. The one thing I knew is that love would conquer all – love them and always fight for them. I vowed that I would take them everywhere with me and do everything for them. I also would never let them remember this moment in their lives. They don't.

Trial was to be in the winter. While doing some work over Ron and Cookie's house, I made sure my wife and kids had a home to live in. We had found a townhome in Brownstown Township. Since I had never been in trouble with the law before, I thought we were going to get probation.

Still trying to keep my business going, I kept asking Ron about next year. He kept telling me something big was in the works. I wouldn't have to worry about work, he said. There would be plenty of it. That sounded great.

We were assigned a court-appointed attorney. Katrina ended up getting probation because of the kids. They were not about to lock her up. Although I didn't have a criminal record, I was facing a felony count. That could have been taken care of if I had the $3,500 to repay the would-be owners. I didn't.

The case did not go well. I wished I had had a better attorney. Court-appointed attorneys don't care about you. They only get paid a miniscule amount by the court. This is why they just go along with whatever is happening. Ultimately, this court-appointed attorney did nothing. I felt I knew more than he did. The damage was already done when I finally took over my own case. I thought I did my best and far better than the court-appointed attorney.

The jury was out for about an hour and came back with a verdict. They read the verdict as my heart raced, and my body shook. They found me guilty. My stomach dropped; my body went numb. My

mind was cloudy. I asked the judge to poll the jury in case one of them disagreed. The verdict had to be anonymous. As each of the jurors was polled, I stood there feeling faint. They all said guilty.

I was immediately taken into custody and spent two weeks in jail before being returned for sentencing. I still thought I would get probation. I waited with about 30 other inmates as the court officer called out our names. Finally, I heard my name called. I stood in front of the judge to be judged and punished. My mind was blank. I start to choke and get teary-eyed, as I proceeded to read my apology and my regrets for my actions to the court and to the judge. I pleaded. I cried. I apologize.

None of that was good enough. I knew where I was about to go. I was ordered to spend one year in the county jail with six months suspended. After I repaid the $3,500, I had to pay into a victims' fund and fines. Then, I would have six months suspended with probation.

I felt so ashamed, especially for my children. I didn't blame any-body for what happened. I never look at the negative. I tried to analyze, and figure out why and how I ended up here. I took the negative and made it into a positive by developing a plan.

Nevertheless, jail was hell on earth. I had no life any more. I was no longer free. I had no rights. I was nothing, the nobody I never wanted to be. Negative feelings eat at prisoners. I knew that the love I once knew outside this wall was gone. I couldn't think of time. There is no time. They owned me. The outside world no longer existed, if I ever thought about the outside world at all. The only world was one day at a time. I did as I was told. My only one goal was to stay alive. I was alone and had to deal with this world to get through it. This wasn't the time to be scared. I had to be either a man with no fear or a target. The thing that kept most inmates from

causing trouble was the fact that, if they didn't behave, more time was added to their sentence. However, that penalty wasn't always good enough.

I served four months in jail before being released two months early for good behavior. I didn't get in any trouble. I would've served longer if my uncle hadn't paid the $3500.

Now I was more determined than ever to show the world who I was and what I was capable of creating. The drive inside me to seek fame and fortune never diminished. I had to prove to myself that sheer will and perseverance will achieve any goal. I wanted to be different, try to achieve greatness and separate myself from everyone else.

I had to overcome every obstacle and to learn that with every risk comes sacrifice, and with every sacrifice, there are consequences.

Becoming successful is the act of trying to improve upon the things you are already doing. It requires growing; developing and accepting bigger and greater challenges; of not being afraid of making mistake; of suffering a setback or caring what other people think of you or of failing. It's trying to be the very best you can be. You just keep going, improving each and every time until you reach your goal.

I always found a way to come away with something good and meaningful under any circumstances. It's called learning a hard lesson. I would not let history repeat itself. To me, this is taking steps backwards. That's not the route to becoming successful and achieving my goals.

In the past, I was doing things for other people. Now, I was going to do it for me and my kids. I didn't have an exact plan, I had passion. I had determination. But, most of all, I think I was pissed off. I was determined to show the world I could not be broken.

I was about to find out what I was really made of, which would push me to near brink of insanity. I would live through it. Why? Because I lived in hell when I was a kid and had no choices I was so young. I was an adult now; I can make choices. I controlled my destiny. I exuded positive feelings and attracted positive people. I surrounded myself with people who were also goal oriented. Some were faced with some of the same things I was facing. I communicated with them. I learned from them and their mistakes

First, I had to get rid of the anchors dragging me down. My grandfather picked me up at the jail on a rainy day. I wore a monitoring device that allowed me to go out at only certain times of the day. It was like home jail. I reported to a probation officer once a month.

Katrina wasn't there, of course. Britney was in kindergarten; Nicole, preschool. Blake was still at home. While they were away, I found some lingerie lying around the house and discovered that my wife had been sleeping with some of my former employees.

I also had to face my Uncle Charley. He gave me a long, stern lecture. That meant he cared. I was old enough to take it.

Despite everything, I remained convinced that I could accomplish great things. I realized things looked pretty dismal for me, but I knew I could get out of it. My credo was that, even if I fell along the way. I would never give into life. I stick to the plan. There was always a way to overcome any setback, and the will to do so has always been there. Things started to work out. My aunt needed some landscaping done. I worked off the debt to her and Uncle Charley that way. After that, a decade would elapse before I saw them again. Despite that, my aunt and uncle were always there for me, especially when I needed them the most. I wanted to show them that all the lectures and all the time they had sat down with me meant something. I wanted them to be

proud of me. However, until I proved everyone wrong, I wouldn't see them again.

In 1994, Katrina filed for divorce. My 10-year marriage was over.

I was 33 years old with three children. I had no job. No money in the bank. I still had six months of probation left. I had no lawyer. I just didn't care. I had to find a way. I never gave up. A door opened. I was allowed to work while on probation. At the same time, Ron Bleckman bought a Ford dealership in Northville, Michigan. Soon thereafter, I met Bob Stewart, head of the service department. Bob and I then negotiated a contract with Ron to remodel the service area at the dealership and take care of the buildings and property. Ron had promised something big. He had come through. Now, it was my turn to prove I deserved his confidence.

CHAPTER 17

Ron, under our new agreement, I would be paid a weekly salary as a contractor, no matter if I worked there or not. Unfortunately, although I was making big money, I was sending Katrina a big check for child support. I was also growing weary of missing my kids. It started to eat me up inside.

Whenever I would see the kids, Katrina would always try to get me in trouble with the police. One time, she accused me of grabbing her breast while we were exchanging the kids. Another time, she claimed I broke the court order by arriving late. Eventually, we had to exchange the kids at the Police Department. That still didn't end the harassment. I was falsely arrested one late night at the dealership for stealing a car. It was my own car that she reported stolen. My encounters with the police would grow. We would be on a first-name basis. They all knew me, and I knew them. I wasn't afraid. Nobody would tell me what to do or how to do it. I would just do the right thing and continue to write that check every month.

On the other hand, I heard stories from the kids about guys coming over Katrina's house. She couldn't hide anything from them.

When they were with me, the kids said a 13-year-old kid frequently babysat them all night. They described drinking and smoking. I could not tolerate that kind of behavior around my children.

In late 1995, Katrina finally got her divorce. I received joint legal custody of the kids, but Katrina was given physical custody. Since I didn't have any credit, I was living in a three-bedroom suite at Ramada in Southfield and understood that I couldn't care for the children there. That was one of the hardest things I had to accept.

Finally, one night, working late at the dealership, I will never forget looking up at the clock. It was three o'clock in the morning. I was talking to my friend Bob Stewart on the phone. I suddenly realized all the work, all the money meant nothing without my kids. Something came over me that night. I felt I could give them some very important things that Katrina could not: guidance; discipline and structure; the drive to succeed; and the tools they would need to survive life and become successful. Most of all, I could offer them unconditional love and compassion. If I couldn't fight for my own kids, how could I ever dream of helping others?

From that point, my purpose and meaning focused on someone other than myself. I would no longer do anything for material gain or money, unless it would help others, not me. Now, everything was for my kids. They were my purpose

I knew getting custody of the children would cost a lot of money. I didn't care. Three months after Katrina was awarded physical custody of our children, I hired some of the top attorneys in the state. If I was going to fight, I was fighting with the best. I spared no expense. I was sticking up for my kids because they couldn't. I even hired private detectives to investigate her every move and to protect the kids.

November 15, 1995, we were both back in court for a custody hearing based on my emergency motion. The judge would decide whether or not, the children should be removed from Katrina and given to me. The testimony was lurid. A 13-year-old girl said she would babysit daily for the children.

She stated that, on one occasion. Katrina came home with three men, went upstairs and made a pornographic film. The girl was asked to have sex with these men and Katrina, and she said, she was offered alcohol and drugs. She further testified she saw Katrina in bed with two men and a camera. She said she saw Katrina hit Blake with a belt on the bottom and called him a bastard. She stated Katrina left her with no telephone number where she could be reached in the event of an emergency.

This testimony corroborated statements made by my daughter, Britney, and contradicted Katrina's claims that Britney misunderstood the events that evening. Custody was changed to me based on the sworn testimony, not mere allegations. This testimony corroborated by my daughter, Britney, contradicted Katrina's testimony and assertion that Britney misunderstood the events that evening.

The decision came quickly. I was temporarily given full custody with a final judgment to be rendered later. That didn't deter Katrina. She wanted those hefty child-support payments. Eventually, she would go through about four different attorneys by the time the battle ended. In fact, she wouldn't stop until Blake turned 18. If I had known then what was about to happen, I still would have fought her. My kids were too important to surrender.

For 18 months I underwent many police meetings and reports, made many court appearances, because of repeated, false and unsubstantiated reports to the Department of Social Services; and endured

multiple psychological evaluations with my whole family. It was almost like the courts were telling me that, if I wanted these children, I was going to go through a lot to be awarded full custody. I even paid for Katrina's psychological evaluations, because she had no money.

The kids and I first stayed at the hotel. I drove them back and forth to school and picked them up after school. Then, I took them to daycare and then go back home. Meanwhile, I worked all over the state. Every day, day after day. Since daycare was expensive, I traded some remodeling at some of the daycare centers in lieu of cash. That eased some of the financial burden. I kept going, daily showing the court that the father of these three children cared about nothing else. There were no women, no drinking, no partying or staying out late. I was just doing in my heart what I felt was right.

Friends, professionals and business owners wrote letters to the court supporting my character and demeanor. In those days, it was very rare for a father to seek custody of his children. But, I was determined to be one of the first. Over time, I started to gain the respect from friends, neighbors and acquaintances. They thought that I was doing the right thing.

I realized throughout the course of the divorce and custody battle that I was not the only one enduring such trials. Other people made it through despite similar stories and the same heartaches and pains, and the distressing worries. I got to know many of them. Some of their stories were as bad as mine or even worse. I listened, and we touched each other's hearts, supporting one another. They were inspiring. It was so motivating to know I was not the only one. We are all human: heart, soul and mind. We all have troubles, but we are a compassionate people. Most of us can relate. Talking to other

people who have experienced the same pain somewhat eases the stress. We had something in common. I realized that someone cared enough about me to share feelings and emotions. That helped me through the tough times and kept me sane.

Eventually I found an Apartment in Northville. Before I could rent, I had to explain the situation to the manager. I had no prior rental history, or any good credit. This woman believed enough in me to take a chance on me. I could tell she had a heart. She showed me compassion that day. I refused to let her down. My kids were enrolled in the Northville schools, which were ranked in the top five in the country academically. Northville then was one of the fastest growing communities in the country, a prestigious and prosperous area. I would be close to work, too.

I signed up all the kids for soccer. They all excelled in the sport. Britney and her team won two championships. They all played for a few years and then got interested in baseball. Britney led her team to two Northville Township championships.

Nicole came in a close second. Blake also shined in baseball and went to win a championship with his team – a chip off the old bloke. I still am so proud of them all.

Finally, on July 22, 1997, Judge Sharon A. Stone issued a 13-page opinion that granted me permanent physical custody of all three children.

Katrina's vindictive plotting and scheming would only get worse from that day forward. She wanted me in jail; that's the only way she thought the kids would ever end up with her again. In a way, she proved to be right.

I had exhausted all my savings and spent everything that I had to do what I believed was the correct way to go. I was never afraid. I

knew what I was capable of, even after letting go of everything and digging myself into a hole again. My kids were all that mattered. None of this was their fault. Besides, money should have nothing to do with doing what's right and just.

I finally filed for bankruptcy. At this point in my life, I knew that many of the wealthiest and most famous people had gone bankrupt, sometimes more than once: Henry Ford, Donald Trump and Larry King, to name a few. Even Abraham Lincoln had. If someone that well off can get into trouble, it can happen to anyone. I was not ashamed. Bankruptcy laws were created to address financial problems and give anyone a chance to get a fresh start, put affairs back on track and gain control of finances. I was willing to take advantage of them.

I wasted no time in reestablishing my credit. It would take me two years to restore my credit to an impeccable rating. Then, I could buy anything I wanted. However, I only bought something that became an asset and made me money.

Before I bought anything, I would ask myself, if this would bring me closer to achieving my goal of being self-sufficient. I still remembered to reward myself for accomplishments. You can do the same thing: go out to dinner, sharing a beautiful romantic evening with significant other, spend a night at the movies, escape to a lake under a shady tree on beautiful sunny day and dream. Let yourself go, fantasize and bring that dream to reality. Realize anything is possible: the bigger the sacrifice, the bigger the reward.

I had no credit cards and haven't since 1987. I pay cash. If I wanted something large, I would take out loans – for a yacht, rv's, exotic cars, business equipment, trucks and more – and pay them off before the note was due. I would buy cars, trucks, limousines and almost anything else for a little money, restore them and then flip

them for profit. I paid off the bad debts on my credit reports and had them removed. I rose above the bankruptcy rating. It was an astonishing task, and I did it. I saved money.

Banks never helped me in the past. Now, I had something they wanted – money and lots of it. I have never liked banks, but I used them to my advantage through the many loans.

By 2000, I was ready to buy a house. I looked at a few homes, but didn't like them. I wanted to have a lot of property. I looked in the country, outside Northville. Now, the area is all built up, but then it was rural. I found 1.5-acre home with three bedrooms, one and a half bath with an attached two-car car garage at the intersection of 8mile and Haggerty. I'll never forget walking the property and through the home, Lots of work needed to be done to develop the property. It was hilly with tons of trees that I would have to remove. I would have to gut the whole house down to the studs, remodel, rebuild and expand. I got goose bumps all over my body. I knew this was the place. I could see the potential. This was where I would fulfill my dream and create my "Dynasty." I was about to build a paradise. I was sure I would need five years to finish it.

I was 39 years old. Britney was 14, and Nicole, 11. Blake was 8 years old. We all worked together as a family to turn this house into our Eden. If I weren't a workaholic back then, I surely became one now. I used all the building, architectural designing, landscape and construction skills I had accumulated over a lifetime and focused them on the house. I worked around the clock, purchasing all the materials wholesale through my companies. I ran my businesses by day and built my estate at night and on weekends. If necessary, I would contract for outside labor, but the kids and I provided most of the labor.

There was no time for anything else, but home construction, sports for the kids and school. Only during Christmas, Easter, and midwinter breaks would we get away. I always took the kids to Florida, where we would go camping, fishing, and boating in our sport fishing yacht, cruise the Intracoastal, visit all the exciting harbors and docks as well as Disneyworld, Universal Studios, Busch Gardens and other Florida theme parks.

In time, I was able to take a $200,000 home with 1,800 sq. ft. of living space and turned it into a sprawling 4,800 sq. ft. estate with a 2400 sq. ft. guest house and a six-car garage.

You might enjoy a tour. As you drove toward the house, you could not help but notice four massive brick columns and four entry gates. There's one pair by each entrance. Your car will pass over 15,000 sq ft. of brick, which leads into a circular drive and then into a massive landing strip-like driveway that takes you down to the guesthouse. There's a six-car heated garage and a 1,200 sq. ft. upstairs studio with full kitchen and a full bath lined with granite walls.

The main house; Just outside the great room, there's a brick patio and a pergola overhead. As you enter the room from the driveway, you'll step onto hardwood floors, and see an antique wall unit. A baby grand player piano stands on a Persian rug. When you play, it's like being at a symphony as the fireplace roars, creating the mood for that evening. The state-of-the-art kitchen features stainless steel Jenn-Air appliances and a glass cooking top, as well as custom-made, white cherry cabinets with Esmeralda green granite countertops, pantry and bar with handcrafted crown moldings and marble floors. An island in the middle holds an arsenal of chef's tools. I built an addition with sunroom, marble floors and Roman columns, attached to a sprawling 1,200 square-foot deck.

Off the deck, there's a full bath entering the great room, with tumbled marble floors and walls. A living room, dining room, and library contain oak hardwood floors, and handcrafted crown and base moldings. Upstairs, you'll find an office, two bedrooms, and a full bath with a double vanity, with granite, and floors and walls done in marble. The 500 square-foot master bedroom comes with vaulted ceilings, tropical fans and a view that's priceless. The master bathroom contains solid cherry cabinets, stainless steel sinks and faucets attached to granite tops, an exotic marble floor and walls designed to resemble a forest.

The lowest floor includes a bedroom, a full kitchen, and a full bath with two shower heads, white and cobalt blue tile on the walls and ceiling with glass-etched tile to resemble water along the perimeter, with whitewashed hardwood floors throughout.

Just off the kitchen, you walk through to two swinging glass doors entering the Jacuzzi filled with exotic trees and plants. From there, you can stroll through the French doors onto the brick patio and into what would resemble a park. That route will lead you to the pool with beautifully landscaped gardens and flowing waterfalls. Granite patios and walkways surround the pool.

By this time, you should be fascinated, caught up with beauty and sheer magnitude of the amount of work that has been done to this masterpiece. But, you're not done. Continue on through the exotic gardens that are laced with beautiful flowers and ornamental trees. Follow the brick trail past boulders with hundreds of pine trees lining the perimeter of the property for privacy. You'll come upon the man-made pond, with a lighted fountain that sprays water up to 35 ft into the air.

Surrounded by boulders and flowering shrubs, the pond is stocked with Koi fish worth thousands of dollars. It lights up at night

in a display that compliments park lights placed throughout the gardens.

I said I would finish in five years, but we actually completed the work a year early. The property jumped in value to well over $1 million. Don't get the wrong impression. The transformation was not easy by any means. I don't just mean the labor.

During construction, cops were called to the house nearly every day for something. The neighbors apparently were getting jealous. On one occasion, probably the most memorable, I recall coming home to find 400 tons of boulders dumped along the front of the house I bought. They created a mountain alongside the road roughly 260' x 20' by 4' high. They would be placed alongside the berms, eventually creating a retaining wall around the perimeter of the backyard. I saw five cop cars and five county dump trucks with a front end loader and another on its way. They were prepared to haul off all the rocks. Thousands of dollars would've been lost if the stones had to be moved away from the road. However, I couldn't move that massive mountain in one day or even two days. We had a long discussion before the county officials ended up pushing the boulders further into my yard with their big front end loader.

Problems also existed within the family. Amid all the constructing, designing, building and landscaping on what was becoming a sprawling estate, Nicole, then a teenager in junior high school, decided she wanted to live with her mother. Naturally, I was reluctant. I recalled how Katrina had behaved and didn't want my daughter exposed to that. Of course, Nicole didn't remember.

As I debated, Nicole began to cause problems. She was becoming another David, making sure her siblings were miserable. She wouldn't do anything to help and continually confronted me. I would never

respond. The idea of abusing my kids in any way never occurred to me. I loved and fought for them way too much to have ever wanted to hurt them in any way. On the other hand, Nicole pushed my tolerance to the limit. She was mean, vulgar, spiteful and, most of all lazy. She wanted to live with her mother and was going to do everything to make sure she got her way.

I was very disappointed with her. While she was being obnoxious, her mother was constantly barraging me with her hidden agendas, scheming, plotting and planning to try to put me in jail. That was a bad combination. Fortunately, Nicole was a very smart and gifted child who was always getting A's and B's in school. I didn't know if she would continue her studies under Katrina's lax supervision. I always had the utmost love and affection for my kids and concern about their lives. As a result, I didn't want my daughter with my ex-wife.

Finally, one day, however, I had enough. Nicole was only hurting her brother and sister, and constantly getting into fights with them. I told her to pack her bags and took her to her mother's house. As you can tell, this was a hard decision for me, but I did not want to return to court or go through any motions. I loved her too much for that. My decision was the right thing to do. This was what she wanted.

In some ways, I could understand her desire to leave. Was I a strict disciplinarian? Yes. Maybe too much so. However, I believe kids need structure and guidance. I am their father first and foremost; their friend, second. Whether they knew or not, the discipline was for their own good. Not a day ever went by without me telling them that I loved them. Still, my kind of strict upbringing could lead to rebellion.

Nevertheless, I would not have changed my approach. Not have a father figure, or, for that matter, a mother who demonstrated any-

thing resembling parenting, I had to learn on my own. I concluded that, in general, to follow common sense whether my decision turned out right or wrong.

I realized that what I did as a parent was instilled in my children. So, I was a very strict and very protective, always their father and the parent that I never had. As a result, I taught my kids how to be independent, even if that meant they rebelled.

My thought was that, in case I didn't live long enough to see them graduate and become successful, I was going to groom them to become driven like their father. It did not matter to me if they liked me or loved me. They didn't have a choice. I had a job to do: teach them; and give them the tools they would need to survive life, have careers and become successful.

With Nicole now living with her mom, work continued at the house. Blake now was 13. Since he was older and bigger, we were able to do much more together. I had started work at his age, so did he, becoming active in my company. Britney was 16, becoming a woman. She, too, would be working outside the house soon.

Unfortunately, the timing was not the best. The economy was starting to slow down. Ron started having problems at the dealership and was not selling enough cars to pay his bills. I was slowing down, too. More than three decades of lifting, pounding, carrying and working when I should have been sleeping was taking a toll on my body.

My life was about to change again.

CHAPTER 18

The changes began when my past made a cameo appearance in my life. On October 6, four days before my birthday, my brother David was killed, burned up in a tanker accident that destroyed the I-75 and I-94 interchange in Detroit. He was 40 years old. He went out like he lived.

His death was the symbol of the seismic shifts about to take place in my life. Five life-changing events hit me all at once. Somehow, I knew they were coming. I could sense them. Just as I knew what would happen when my mother looked for me in the basement so many years ago, I knew that my immediate future was going to be very different from the present. I didn't know why: maybe what happened to David or the constant pressure from Katrina or even the neighbors' sniping. Or, maybe, God whispered in my ear again.

Somehow, I knew it was all coming to a head.

I wondered if I could handle it, but was determined to try. Traumatic events help anyone become a person and realize how strong he or she really is. I am a fighter, a survivor, and I refuse to let life destroy me. I will conquer whatever life has to throw at me and move

forward, to the next level. Fear and failure are never options. I will not run. I will persevere.

On the other hand, what eventually happened was essentially chaos.

For starters, my companies and Ron's Ford Dealership were not doing well. By 2005, the recession was spreading across the country like a dark stain. Ron was borrowing money to keep the dealership afloat and make the payroll. I had faith in him that everything would work out.

After knowing him for nearly 20 years, through countless projects and working on his personal homes, I had no reason not to trust him. He treated me like the son he and his wife never had.

He asked me to loan him a couple hundred thousand dollars to save the dealership. I agreed. I thought that by giving him the money I was also helping myself. If the dealership stayed afloat, I would be saving my contract to maintain buildings. The logic made sense.

I had the funds because I was in the process of selling some off some of my assets: my yacht, two moving trucks and a Ford truck. Instead of replacing them, I went ahead and loaned Ron the money. I trusted that he would pay me back, as he promised.

At the same time, I did more than $100,000 worth of work on his property. He had more than that 100 elm trees that were killed by a disease that first invaded the United States back in the 1930s. It had slowly spread until it devoured the elms in Michigan. Ron needed the dead trees removed throughout the property. I worked through the winter, driving the tractor through the snow, cutting down trees and hauling the wood to a special dumping ground where they were chipped and burned. When the project was finished, his land looked like a tornado had swept across it.

Despite everything, Ron eventually lost the dealership. He owed me hundreds of thousands of dollars for both the loan and the yard work that he could not pay. When I tried to reach him to discuss the debt, he started ignoring my phone calls. In the end, I had no choice. I had to sue my best friend, my father figure, and his wife. They were the only people I ever trusted. I felt betrayed and, in time, would receive only a fraction of what he owed me. I did learn a lesson, such as it is.

People will say whatever they can to convince you to loan them money when they're desperate. My advice, which was painfully learned: Don't ever loan anyone money, unless you have it to lose.

While my relations with Ron and Cookie deteriorated beyond repair, Britney started acting very strangely whenever she would come back from visiting her mother. Her behavior wasn't just bad; it was unconscionable. Every Christmas, we had been going to Florida. Christmas 2005 was different. I sat down and talked to her, finding out why she was behaving so oddly, but she wouldn't tell me why. Then, one day, I came home from work. She wasn't there. She was at her mother's. Katrina had picked her up from school. I called and spoke to my daughter. Britney said she wasn't going to come home. I couldn't figure out why.

The next day, the police contacted me. They needed a statement from me concerning Britney. I still didn't know what was going on. I knew I hadn't done anything wrong. So, I went without my attorney, gave the police my statement and left.

The next day, I was being charged with a felony. Britney claimed I had fondled her, while Blake, she and I were walking upstairs. I was appalled. This was serious. I was facing 25 years in jail on a felony charge.

I knew Katrina must have had something to do with this. However, I also knew Britney had a boyfriend who lived close to her mother's

home. I figured my daughter must have been coaxed by Katrina so she could leave my custody to live near her boyfriend. I could just imagine how Katrina made Britney feel. After all, Britney had testified against Katrina and cost her custody. Britney was so young then and must have felt guilty to have hurt her mother. This charge had Katrina's name written all over it, full of her desire for revenge and spite. I don't blame Britney. She was just a pawn in this vicious game.

In a way, I was not worried. Blake had walked up the stairs beside me. He knew that the allegations simply were not true. He would later give a deposition in my behalf.

However, I would have never allowed Britney or any of my kids for that matter to see or have a boyfriend or girlfriend until they were older. I raised all my kids to go to college have careers and a large bank account before they ever would get involved or even think of starting a family. And Katrina knew it.

She continued to attack me through the courts. Trying to remove my son from my custody, Katrina filed papers with Judge Nancy L. White, who knew our case from previous court appearances. In her brief, Katrina claimed I was an unfit father because there were charges pending against me for a felony concerning my daughter. That approach simply did not work. Katrina would try a few times, making a series of false accusations. The judge easily realized what my ex-wife was trying to do on each occasion, and Blake remained with me.

While waiting to go to trial, tired, beaten, stressed and sore, I installed the four massive tumble block columns that would hold my entry gates, by hand with the help of my son. The work was the only way I knew to relieve stress and anger. It helped me analyze the situation and to put things into perspective. I was in control, not out-

of-control. Sadly, this was to be the last time that I would be able to perform such heavy labor. My back balked at the task. I was in so much pain and could barely walk. As I went to the doctor and learned the bitter news: I would either have to find a new profession or take the risk of further hurting my back. If that happened, I might never walk again. My lifting days were over. Although I could still lift a little, I couldn't do at the rate or consistency I had been doing in the past. I needed a new career.

While I was anguishing over my future, the trial was ready to start. By then, my attorney had worked out a plea agreement. We went into a room off to the side of the court room with court officials and my attorney. I read what the prosecutor offered. The state would drop all the charges if I agreed to plead guilty to assault and battery. As punishment, I would be put on reporting probation for a year and not be allowed to have any contact with Britney until she turned 18.

I balked immediately. I had never hit my daughter or any of my kids other than grounding them or giving them time out in their bedroom when they were younger. I was innocent.

I sat quietly, listening to the prosecutor and my attorney. Many thoughts went through my head. Britney was 16. At 18, she would be an adult and beyond court control anyway. She could move out of my house then, even if I didn't want her to. Also, if I won, I would at best have a sullen, angry teenager living with me for one more year. Besides, the situation would be the same as when she was much younger, only this time she would be testifying against her father instead of her mother. Did I really want her to go through that emotional turmoil again?

Then, too, her sister was already at her mother's house. They could help each other if Katrina began to do anything against one of them.

There was more: what if I was found guilty? I know I'm innocent, but a jury would have to decide, and miscarriages happen. Nothing is 100 percent guaranteed. My attorney didn't have to tell me that. I had gone through a trial before. I could get 25 years in jail. I had already spent too much time there.

Even more of concern was my son. If I were sent away, Blake would lose his father. I knew he was not close to his mother. The episode with the belt and calling him names certainly soured him.

I understood his feelings completely. I hadn't seen my mother in years. With a trial, I wasn't just gambling with my life, but with his. If that happened, Blake would not have his father any more. I could not do that to him. It no longer mattered that I was not guilty. I had to think of Blake first. If it were not for my son, I would have fought and went to trial.

I agreed to plead guilty. I also thanked my attorney. He understood fully well the complete situation. He wasn't just a lawyer; he was a friend who fought for me. When I couldn't struggle anymore, he believed in me. He saved my life that day.

Now, I could focus on rescuing my company. I tried to advertise, but received no response. With the economy collapsing, no one had money to spend on remodeling or beautifying a house or a yard. Houses were depreciating at an astronomical rate, making an investment in the house useless. If any business had shown up, I would have done it despite the risk to my back and health. None did.

I was 43 years old and on the verge of total bankruptcy again.

I was facing foreclosure on my house, which had been a dream of mine and only recently been completed. I was not alone. Many Americans were confronted by the same disastrous situation. Like them, I had hard choices to make. The first was obvious: I put my dream house up for sale. No one was interested.

The second choice was to pay off the mortgage by emptying all of my savings and selling any additional assets. If I did that, however, I would be starting at the bottom again. I wouldn't have any money to invest or to launch another endeavor. Besides, even if I started a business, I couldn't do the heavy lifting or building.

Because of my financial track record, I knew investors who would back me, but with the weak economy and limited business, how could I ever pay them back?

I really thought hard logically and financially about this option, setting my emotions aside. In the end, I said no to investors. That would not be a good option. I did not want to owe anyone a cent ever again.

I made my decision. First, I decided to host a huge party. I had a live band and all the food that any guest could want, and invited family and friends to see the paradise I had created. When the party was over, I took the next step and walked away from my dream home.

I retired, selling off any assets. I even sold a new Harley-Davidson police interceptor motorcycle I had won from the Northville Police Department in a 2004 drawing. My name made it into the local newspapers. What a day that was. I felt vindicated after all the strife and harassment I had endured from the local police. I knew Katrina was the cause. They were only doing their jobs. I really have nothing against them. Some of the Northville police officers are

among the best in the country. When they called me to say I had won the motorcycle, I didn't even believe them. I thought I was going to be arrested again, but was told to go to Sheehan's on Green, a restaurant in Plymouth. Every cop in the town was there. The looks on their faces were priceless. They were all really polite and congratulated me. That was a first.

Then, without regret, I let my property go into foreclosure. I saved more than $700,000 plus interest with this decision. It was the right choice. The estate had depreciated rapidly. It was worth less than what I owed. The equity in the house was lost, and I could never recoup the difference. Despite everything, there was still one more major change to go.

CHAPTER 19

Now, I was unemployed. My two daughters had moved in with my ex-wife. I was responsible for a teenage boy. I was on probation. I didn't have a house or any saleable assets and could not return to my old profession because of my back. Fortunately, I had not lost my ability to adapt or my will to continue, regardless of the situation.

I reinvented myself and financed another pursuit – but in a totally different direction.

In the early 1990s, the Internet first gained a public face, although the basic applications and guidelines that make the Internet possible had already existed for more than two decades. I had an interest in computer technology, and so I purchased my first computer and fiddled around with it. Once again, I found people who understood more than me and learned from them.

In need of a new profession, I turned my attention to becoming a computer entrepreneur as interest in computers swept the country. I became a part of the "next big thing," the worldwide computer networking system known as the Internet.

I found a certain overlap in my skills. In time, using design-skills developed through landscape architecture, and engineering, I would create, develop and launch some of the biggest websites in the world. Essentially, I developed a money-making machine that worked around the clock. I could run my corporation from anywhere in the world, using only a laptop. The business catapulted me into the new age of technology and a whole new realm of making money.

I relied on software developers. I hired a web development firm in Michigan and software engineers from around the globe, including Russia, Hungary, England and the United States. I opened offices and studios in Europe, and in Las Vegas and Detroit. My sites brought people together, networking venues like My Space, Face Book and many others My major competitors are E Harmony.com, Match.com, and Adult Friend Finder.

For the first time, I also saw the world myself. I had been all across the United States moving clients, but had lived only in Michigan, Texas and Florida, and nowhere else. Now, I moved to Las Vegas for two years and then to Europe, traveling to operate studios and offices from there.

I set out on this crusade not knowing the depth of time or money it would require, armed only with the sheer will to succeed. This is one of my greatest challenges and yet one of the most rewarding. I created an executive summary on my company and landed a couple of investors. I then decided to do it on my own. That was harder and took more time, but contained less risk, and I completely owned the company. Later, I took my business public.

During my research and development phase, a beautiful young woman, Cristina Negrila, in Bucharest, Romania, eventually becomes my liaison, running the office and a studio in Europe.

Back in the states, I ran the studio, and formed a group for a show in Las Vegas named the "Dynasty Girls."

I traveled around the world, bringing millions of people together, networking with over 3 million members. The Model's, the studios, streaming videos around the world. Webcams, instant messaging , the travel, producing, writing, and the setbacks. All orchestrated by one man — me.

This is a story that will be told later – another adventure of mine that emerged from temporary chaos.

Meanwhile Blake was still in Northville High School, so he stayed with friends of the family. I kept in contact with him during this time by flying back and forth for weeks at a time.

The situation did not faze him. I believe this was a good experience for him. He has always been a good student academically, and remains polite and courteous. After all, he is a reflection of me. Everyone loves my son. Of course, he had no option. He was going to stay with me rather than live with his mother.

As the Internet flourished, I decided to tell my story. This was part of my overriding passion to help other people, especially kids, who need motivation. I have used seminars and motivational speaking to tell the world about my journey. I also created a printing company. While living in Vegas, I went back and forth to Malibu, California before forming a production company in Hollywood. I called it Shark Reef Productions. Eventually, I want to produce a movie on my life. I started Dynasty International Publishing to print my book.

Everything I learned in my life previously is helping me now. For example, the sales calls I made with my first business taught

me to always look my best. Unfortunately, people invariably judge you by your first appearances: your looks, the way you walk, your smile, the way you speak and carry yourself. That has always bothered me. In the first place, I endured that kind of critical observations when I was covered with acne and was dressed shabbily from living in a car. Yet, I'm the same person now. As far as I'm concerned, no one should judge anyone. No one is better than the other person, no matter who they are or their status in life. Still, people will judge you just as they judged me. Society can either give you fame and fortune or persecute and ridicule you, and give you nothing. That sounds shallow, doesn't it? Unfortunately, that's how society is.

Eventually, I returned to Michigan, where I live now. I bought a condo for my son. In 2008, I returned to doing what I do best: turning someone else's dream into reality. His name is John, and he is in his mid-70s. Before he dies, John wants to create paradise in his backyard with beautiful gardens with flowering ornamental trees, flowing rivers, streams and waterfalls, and ponds. The property would be filled with brick patios and walkways to take visitors through the gardens. I have been helping John with the help of my son, now 18 and needing a job. Who better to give him one than me? Besides, I've undergone more changes than John's backyard.

There was one more to go. The last step seems the smallest, but it turned out to be monumental.

I never had a problem with the way I looked. No one would probably know or even notice because of my demeanor, character and confidence. However, I really didn't like the way my teeth appeared. I searched for three years to find the right dentist to do the job. I almost gave up.

None of them convinced me that they could reconstruct my whole mouth, raise my bite and crown all of my teeth. Because of my tooth problems over the years, I had a considerable amount of experience with dentists. As far as I'm concerned, most of them can't be trusted. They only seem to care about money, not their patients.

Because my ability to speak is so important, I had to be convinced that, if something happened during the procedure, the dentist would know how to correct the problem. I would not be able to get my teeth back once the dentist began drilling. I trusted nobody, and I mean nobody. I wouldn't let anybody into my life. I was very private. By now, considering everything that had happened to me, I am sure you could understand why.

One summer, I came across a dentist named Dr. Cristal in Northville – and no, not Cristal who played the role of Carrington's wife on the prime time television soap opera " Dynasty". Although the same name is very fitting for her: gorgeous , stunning, professional, and driven. I scheduled a consultation with her and put her through an extensive range of questions. No lawyer or psychiatrist was more thorough during my legal issues. Are you going to raise my bite? I asked her. What if there's a problem? How would you correct it? I wanted guarantees. Even though I've met a lot of people through my multiple business deals, I had never found someone like Cristal with such energy, enthusiasm and confidence. She just kept firing back answers at lightning speed. She never faltered, hesitated or stuttered, all sure signs of problems. I make everyone nervous, but not her. I loved our conversation. For the first time, I met someone that wasn't afraid to take on a challenge. She was confident and as solid as a rock. By the end of the consultation, she had earned my respect. I had found someone I could trust with my teeth.

Once Cristal agreed to do the work, I did not interfere. Throughout my business career, I learned that, if you hire someone to do a job, always make him feel that you trust and believe in him. That person will do the best possible job and will go out of his way for you because he wants you to believe in him. Don't pressure. Be positive and encourage him, and praise him or her. That way, everything will go well. You trust his sincere effort: a real win-win situation.

For two months, I had to wear a device to raise my bite. In late September, I arrived in Cristal's office for the first procedure. She filed down the tops of all my teeth in preparation for porcelain crowns. As I sat in her chair for more than eight hours, I was amazed at her skill and patience. She performed with such precision without a flaw. Amazingly, I felt no pain at all. She took impressions for temporary crowns, and I was done. I was scheduled to return in five weeks.

During that time, Cristal stopped by John's house to see the waterfalls. She wanted to see the progress because she had a house in California that needed to be upgraded. I agreed to look at it. She was so energetic, so glowing and so happy. Her happiness wasn't from business, but rather what I associated with friendship or feelings toward a boyfriend. She made me feel good. I felt something, but I didn't know what. Remember, I hadn't dated for years and had not had much to do with women since Katrina.

We talked over next week or so before coming to an agreement on redesigning the waterfalls behind her home in Malibu California,. I pack up my tools and went there while Blake stayed here to take care of John's project. While in California, I constantly would talk to him about his progress.

Then I get a text message from Cristal: Wish I were there with you. I didn't know how to respond to that. I didn't know if I should

respond at all. After all, she was married. Eventually, I wrote back innocuously, saying that it looks like thunderstorms are rolling in here and left it at that. I knew something was happening, but still didn't know how to take it.

Soon after, I went; I came back to Michigan before returning to Malibu a couple of weeks later to finish. While in Michigan, I winterized John's waterfalls. Meanwhile, things were heating up with Cristal. She sent me a seductive text message. At this point, I realized she liked me. However, I wasn't about to break up her marriage. I wasn't like my younger brother. I called her and asked her if I were hallucinating or if this was for real. Cristal said it was. I didn't lose control. I keep an open mind and asked myself how this could ever lead to anything.

I finally sat down in her dental chair for the crowns. I remained in awe of her professionalism and skill, and knew I had chosen the right dentist. The crowns were perfect.

Afterwards, she invited me to lunch. We walked down the street to the deli called Mattie's and shared a sandwich. She watched me and couldn't believe I wasn't feeling any pain. That wasn't really what was on her mind. She told me that she liked my energy, the way I think and the way I look. There was no point in being shy. I told her I felt the same way about her. As I looked into her eyes, I felt I could see her soul. I could feel her pain. I could see her beauty. I could also see the little girl inside the woman. I felt as though I had known her all my life. At that moment I saw her as the Angel that would stand alongside me.

I was not interested in a friendship, let alone a relationship with any woman. Still this feeling deep down in my soul was growing stronger. I had experienced relationships in the past where I would

do everything for my girlfriends, making their dreams come true.I was always the rescuer, giving all of me, treating them like queens. They did not love me, but loved what I could do for them.

Cristal talked to me about her marriage. I was uneasy as I listened. Cristal was a beautiful woman who was in pain. She just wanted to be loved, held, fulfilled and cherished, but I refused to take advantage of her vulnerability. She was hurt and empty. As I sat, listening to her describe her dysfunctional marriage, the verbal and mental abuse inflicted upon her by her husband Tony. His physical hygiene was appalling as she described him never taking showers, always smelling like a sewer as he forced himself upon her; with no respect to her as a woman. Even a 13 year old knows where a bar of soap and running water are. There were many occasions he threatened her with vulgar language; keeping her in fear using their kids against her.

On one occasion the vulgar and unconscionable and quite honestly very disturbing behavior, Tony acting out against a wall thrusting himself against it; while making obscene gestures accusing Cristal of some kind of sexual misconduct with her son while the kids were in the house that morning. A very disturbed man her husband. In fear for her life I called the police out to their house after she escaped, practically unclothed and no shoes from her husband bashing her with a barrage of vulgar language while trying to force himself upon her.

As she filed for divorce the abuse only got worse. He threatened to take everything and destroy her business she had worked so hard for all her life; the world she created for her family. Tony continued to use derogatory abusive language in front of the kids. She was treated like she was worthless. One would think this man had some kind of intelligence being a chemist at "BASF" rather than a person

with a serious mental disorder. Cristal built a successful business, is a devoted mother, and a wife for 17 years. She loves her children dearly, they are everything to her. He knew how to hurt here through the kids. How much abuse should one be objected to before they gain enough courage to get out? Now he would take from her the money he never earned, nor would have in his lifetime.

The untold secrets she dare not tell in fear of the threats, false accusations, slander to her neighbors, friends and family about her and I, are still kept within her. The courage and strength she would have to find deep down within herself will lead her to find her own identity. Anyone man or woman who can stand up to their abuser despite what other people think deserves respect. We all have been there; in one way or another.

We had to ask ourselves and search our feelings. You analyze, you ask, why, is this sensation too good to be true? You don't find the answer logically or elsewhere. Then you search your heart and soul, God's world. In your very existence, your very being, you will find the answer. If this is true love you share together, like we are sharing now, you are destined to be one in heart, mind and soul. You not only feel it, you know without a doubt that you will be together.

I went back to California the next day, but I spoke with her daily. We missed each other. I wondered if, after all these years, I had finally found the one woman who could love me and be loved in return. Still, with my history, I hesitated to open my heart and mind. Besides, we could not really be together unless she was divorced. She wanted to get one.

I did nothing to encourage her. I would not bare my heart unless she was single again. I was not going to take a chance of exposing myself only to have something go wrong. In time, when her divorce

was finalized, all of the hardship, turmoil and heartache from the past was wiped away.

Soon we were in each other's arms, sharing, laughing and loving. We spent every day like that, cherishing each moment we spend together. No one has ever touched me the way Cristal has. I feel the energy that flows through her as she touches me and know she loves me. When I hold her in my arms, softly caress her face and look into her eyes, I see and feel her love. I see the world through her eyes and her eyes everywhere in the world. I have never felt love like that before. Nor had she.

We hold one another, lying in bed together, with her lips like wine, her skin so soft and her beauty so alluring. We caress one another, feeling every heartbeat, beating as one, as every pulse sends shivers down our spine, with every gasping breath telling each other we love each other. We look into each other's eyes, adoring each other, respecting each other, worshiping each other, like there was never going to be tomorrow. Our passion will never break. She is my goddess, and I will always love her. I live and breathe with her every heartbeat.

We will never stray from each other. We are one with one mind, and one soul, one heart beating together as one. I feel blessed and privileged to love this beautiful, astonishing woman, and blessed to be able to experience a love so deep, so powerful and so giving. If not for her, I would have not experienced this love in my lifetime. I remain humbled. She completed me.

Over the years, I got to know myself, what I was made of, my, drive, my ambition and my aspirations. Still, there was always something missing. All I created, built, achieved and acquired didn't ease the reality that I was alone and had no one to share my passion with,

my life, my adventure, I was empty inside lonely and alone, waiting for the one. Cristal felt the same way.

Brought together by an indescribable force, our two empty souls filled with love and passion. This is a gift that only a few can describe and understand. I will never take her love for granted. I cherish the sheer and utter magnitude of strength she gives me. It is so incredible because it is rare. It's the fairy tale that only God can grant, a blessing and power that will live and flourish in each of us for eternity.

Our relationship is still flourishing. Our love is greater than any other power in this world. It gives us a sense of purpose. We are drawn to each other. We are meant to accomplish far greater things in this world. We feel the power and capability of doing so, together. I feel God has given us this power together to help others.

We have not gotten married. I don't care. God lives in everyone. God didn't write laws on marriage; man did. Actually, men want to control through fear. Of course, everyone needs hope and someone to believe in. Without hope, there is no life and no reason for being. Without hope, there is fear. Through my faith, God is with me throughout my life. He has saved me. I'm here alive today because of him. He is my faith. He was there when I had no one, the voice that showed me comfort and gave me strength. I do not need a Bible or priests in church to preach to me, He lives in all of us in our minds and in our hearts. He gives us hope. God forgives all. There are no sins in his world. I know the kind gentle, loving God.

He is compassion. He breathes in every heartbeat. He is the spirit that lives on forever. He is the soul and mind of everyone every day. He has the power to forgive. He gives faith. He is the very existence of life, and death. God is not fearful. He lives in the life and soul of every living being. He is the indescribable force that brings empty

souls together and fills them with love. Ask of him, and he will answer. Anything in life that is so unexplainable, so grand, so beautiful, and precious is a gift from God and should not be squandered. I don't fear God. I made it through my childhood because of Him. God brought me and Cristal together and helped us share love.

The depth of our love and the unexplainable powers that drove us both together could only mean one thing: God is here. We love each other and cherish that gift for eternity. I do not have to say anything else.

God has protected me for more than 48 years. I lived through hell on this planet, and He was there. I never asked why I was ever put through the pain and suffering. There was a reason. There was a purpose. I welcomed God. He sat beside me. He comforted me when I was in need and unsure where to turn next.

I fear no evil. That's good, since I've made a lot of mistakes along my path in life. We all make mistakes. We all make choices. There are many difficult decisions to make throughout life. Some are worth fighting for, and some are not, some lead into chaos. But these are some of the defining moments that make you who you are. Most difficult decisions that you have to make in your life can be the most rewarding in the end.

I could have always chosen to be passive and do nothing. Then, the reward would have been nothing. It's the people who are willing to take that risk and face it head on who become extraordinary. They will succeed in life.

I have learned so much more. I am not ashamed of the pain and suffering I had to endure as a child. That made me who I am today. If it weren't for that pain and suffering, I would not have the power and the drive or, most of all, God, faith and love. Without suffering,

there is no feeling of achievement. You must first overcome the suffering. Then, when you have achieved your goal, you will feel a tremendous sense of accomplishment. You must be willing to sacrifice and abandon material things. At any given moment, you must be ready to change and adapt. Fight for what you know is right and feel. Learn from your mistakes and move on. Forgive those who have hurt you in your life and move on. Do not dwell on the past or hold grudges. Let it go. Do not judge. We are all human with feelings and emotions.

No one is better than the other or above, someone else. We are equal. Move on. Success isn't measured by what you have; it's measured by what you go through to get to every little achievement. Strive for success, to achieve your objective.

People in life judge you on what you own or your status in life, but what they don't know is what you went through and what you sacrificed and abandoned to get there. Do not judge, respect.

Be humble and compassionate for the less fortunate. Do not scrutinize, lest you be scrutinized yourself.

That is why I forgave my mother and grandmother. I do not know the path they walked or the sacrifices and choices they had to make, things that they had to abandon to try to give me and my brothers a better life than what they had. I did not know what life had thrown in their path, and sacrifices they made to put food on the table, provide clothing and a roof over our head. I don't know what they had to endure through their life. They did not know what they did to me.

That's also why I have forgiven my children. Parenthood is one of the hardest things I ever did. I can't say that I have been the most exemplary father. I can say my kids were the most important in my

life. They know the love that I have for them. They often gave me that hope and faith so that I could continue living. I'm proud of them all.

They are adults now. I remember when they were so young. They still are in my heart and mind. The best choice I ever made was never looking back. I would not have done anything different with them. I drove them all and disciplined them to be who they are today. I am so proud of them. Britney now works at three different hospitals and graduates from Madonna college in 2010.

She was on the honor roll at Wayne State University and is pursuing her career as an anesthesiologist or a doctorate in nursing. Nicole is also in college, following her sister's footsteps.

Blake is attending college focused on business management, but is thinking about a career in architecture and civil engineering like I once did. In truth, my kids are my greatest accomplishment. They are my pride and joy. Despite everything, they are the greatest reflection of me. I am humbled and grateful through my faith in God that I am able to witness their paths unfold. My door is always open for them, much like my Uncle Charley did for me in the past. My kids call or we have lunch when they seek my advise

I am proud I was born in this life. I thank my mother for that. Otherwise, I would not have experienced the kind of love I have now. That's what makes my life so incredible. Our relationship today is a civil one. She doesn't remember much about the past, and it is probably best she doesn't

Every story has an ending But, in this life, every ending is also a beginning – a journey that never ends. It is the dream that will never die, bringing a new venture, new goals and new mountains to climb. I have always chased the dream. I expected nothing less than success

and was willing to die for it. I never gave up. I have lived and lead an extraordinary and fascinating life, and had fun along the way. My achievements and successes were worth the risk.

I know what God's love and the power of faith have done in my life, and I wrote this book in the hopes that my story will inspire, motivate and move you. I hope it will give you strength to follow your dreams and hope it will give you the courage to make the tough decisions and sacrifices through your quest for success.

> *I pray this account will give you hope and faith, replacing despair; and love and comfort where there was no light. May the paths you choose to follow be successful, and, most of all, may you be blessed and filled with the love and faith of God. May He be by your side, guiding you and giving you the strength to rise above your fears, your enemies, your dilemmas and chaos that may be in your life.*
>
> *A quote from Charles Darwin to remember for our times: "It is not the strongest of the species that survives, nor the most intelligent that survives. It is the one that is the most adaptable to change."*

I remain active. I leave for Europe again in the summer, leaving my son to run the project at Johns, while dreams of Cristal once again fill my heart. I long to be with her and daily await her call. I thrill to hear the love in her voice. After I return to the States, I will train for the next two years, including a six-day mountaineering course through the Cascades near Seattle, Washington. After that, I plan to climb Mount Everest. The course is required before I am

allowed to climb the world's tallest mountain. I've reached higher peaks, but not physically. The journey begins

I will climb for the kids. All the proceeds will be donated to a charity for abused kids.

For every book that is sold, 10% percent of the proceeds will also be donated to charity

If I can help through writing this book and save just one life, inspire just one child and be the inspiration for someone else's dreams, then all that I endured has been worth it.